"Have you ever wondered what your daughter thinks about you? You will be greatly encouraged reading this wonderful book, written by the daughter of my great friend, Harry Dent. Ginny talks about her dad in ways that only a daughter could and tells the wonderful story of how God took this political pioneer—leader of the New Republican party in the South—and turned him into a gentle saint. This was, for me, very moving reading."

Chuck Colson
Founder of Prison Fellowship and Colson Center for Christian Worldview

"Ginny Dent Brant has written a truly remarkable book. Many of us knew Harry S. Dent Sr. as a trailblazing Republican who helped shape the strong conservative base in the South, but that only begins to scratch the surface. In this book we are privileged to gain insight into the touching story of his daughter, Ginny, and their relationship—which reminds me once again of the importance of family, faith in God and living in a free country."

Former Arkansas Governor Mike Huckabee
Host of Fox News Channel's *Huckabee*
Chairman of Huck PAC, a Republican Volunteer Organization

"From his early fight for freedom in the political arena to the spiritual freedom he discovered later in life through his newfound faith in God, Harry Dent was an inspiring leader. Harry was a man who loved God and his country, and *Finding True Freedom* is a moving tribute to the legacy of a lifetime spent in service to both."

US Senator Jim DeMint
Author of *Saving Freedom: We Can Stop America's Slide into Socialism*

"Ginny Brant has written a fascinating story of her father, Harry Dent, inside the Nixon White House and inside the man. As an excellent writer, she interweaves her relationship with him as he moves from a political strategist to a kingdom strategist. Read this book of a loving father-daughter relationship and Ginny's continuing battle for the principles her father fought for."

Dr. Avery Willis
Author of *Masterlife, Day by Day in God's Kingdom* and
The Biblical Basis of Missions
Former Vice President for the International Mission Board of the
Southern Baptist Convention

"Harry Dent worked with presidents and world leaders, but his greatest impact was as a humble servant who helped to lead so many to Christ."

Former Oklahoma Congressman J.C. Watts
Author of *What Color is Conservative?: My Life and Politics*

"Ginny Dent Brant has written an amazing book. She skillfully combines into one story her own wonderful life with the dramatic story of her father. The book is very rich in the political history of the United States between 1970 and 2000. However, the real fascination comes from its spiritual insights. In nine short years Harry Dent did more for the Romanian people than any other American I know. We, the Romanians, treasure his memory, and we thank Ginny for the full story of her father."

Dr. Josef Tson
Former President of the Romanian Missionary Society

"From the early days of Christendom, believers in Christ have struggled to find the proper balance between being "in the world" and "not of the world"—between dedicating their time and effort toward the hoped-for betterment of the present age and rescuing captives from the spirit of this age for a better life in the age to come. Ginny Dent Brant's *Finding True Freedom* narrates a fascinating and intimate insider's perspective of a youth living in the shadows of the halls of secular power-brokering, and a journey toward discovering an entirely new perspective with more transcendent, eternal values. Brant's personal account of the spiritual pilgrimage of her father, former Nixon aide Harry Dent, and her own parallel story, intertwined with his, is punctuated throughout with poignant pictures of the grace of God and thoughtful reflections on those things that, when all is said and done, will truly matter. Her style is easy to read, colorful and never dull. And the message she has to share is one of considerable consequence for the day in which we live."

David Rogers
Senior Editor of the Adrian Rogers Pastor Training Institute
Former Missionary and Author of the blog *Love Each Stone*

"Rarely is such a well-documented book written which so poignantly speaks to the political arena, to family values and to worldwide ministries of eternal significance. A resilient man of strong, unwavering character and conviction, Harry Dent's passion for truth overrides all else. Beware. After perusing the book, one likely will be challenged to reevaluate priorities, aim higher, and invest life and energy in a cause of eternal significance. An excellent book to read and ponder!"

Bobbye Rankin
Wife of President Jerry Rankin of the International Mission Board
of the Southern Baptist Convention

"From the time I was a child, I have had a love of politics. I followed presidential campaigns before there was TV. This book is a fascinating story of a teenager who prayed for her father, a well-known Washington insider, until he received the Lord and his whole life was transformed."

Florence Littauer
Author and Speaker

"My friend, Harry S. Dent, a former top aide of Strom Thurmond and President Richard Nixon, stood for freedom all his life. He played a key role in building the Republican Party in the South and helped Romania recover from the shackles of Communism. This is a must-read for all who value freedom in a day when our freedoms are gradually disappearing."

Roger Milliken
Chairman and former CEO of Milliken & Company, Inc.
Environmentalist

"I came to know Harry Dent when he joined us in an evangelistic mission in Romania in 1990 after Ceausescu had been ousted. His earnest love of the Lord Jesus and of the Romanian people was evident. His daughter Ginny Dent Brant has captured the life of her Father in a way that will introduce you to the miracle of a living memory. His story will bless you."

John Guest
Pastor of Christ Church at Grove Farm, Sewickley, Pennsylvania
President of John Guest Evangelistic Association

"Harry Dent was obviously one of Richard Nixon's most highly trusted friends. This became apparent to me when he called me at my Seattle home in early 1973 to pass along an appeal from my brother to enter the campaign for the 2nd district congressional seat against the incumbent Lloyd Meads. I had met Harry only once that I can remember, but receiving such a personal call to convey a message from my brother—via his close friend Harry Dent—proves my first sentence!"

Edward Nixon
Brother of President Richard Nixon and coauthor of *The Nixons*

"Ginny winsomely writes of a Columbia I remember during both high school and college days. She writes with an insider's view of the Nixon White House, and with tenderness of her father, whom I admired as a teenager. Bryant and I also remember when Harry Dent preached in our church of the change Christ had made in his life."

Anne Wright
Bryant Wright
Author of *Seeds of Turmoil*
President of the Southern Baptist Convention 2010
Pastor of Johnson Ferry Baptist Church, Marietta, Georgia

"In this page-turning, daughter's-eye view of Harry Dent's rebirth, there is the equally moving parallel story of Ginny's own journey of faith, from childhood to womanhood, through her political and personal turmoil during the Watergate era and beyond."

Mari Maseng Will
Assistant to the President and Communications Director for
President Ronald Reagan

FINDING TRUE FREEDOM

From the White House to the World

GINNY DENT BRANT

CLC PUBLICATIONS

Fort Washington, PA 19034

God Bless —
Ginny
Matt 6:33

Published by CLC Publications

U.S.A.
P.O. Box 1449, Fort Washington, PA 19034

GREAT BRITAIN
51 The Dean, Alresford, Hants. SO24 9BJ

AUSTRALIA
P.O. Box 469, Kippa-Ring QLD 4021

NEW ZEALAND
10 MacArthur Street, Feilding

Printed in the United States of America
18 17 16 15 14 13 12 11 10   1 2 3 4 5 6

ISBN-13 (paperback): 978-1-936143-09-2
ISBN-13 (hardcover): 978-1-936143-10-8

Unless otherwise noted, Scripture quotations are from the Holy Bible, New International Version, © 1973, 1978, 1984 by International Bible Society. Used by permission of Zondervan Bible Publishers.

Italics in Scripture quotations are the emphasis of the author.

DEDICATION

To my husband and best friend, Alton,

who has stood with me throughout my journey in life
for forty years.

To my mother, Betty Dent,
who encouraged me in my journey toward true freedom,
even when my father did not.

To my father, Harry Dent,
a wonderful father who always loved me
and only wanted the best for me,
even when we disagreed.

To both of my parents,
whose willingness to openly share their lives to help others
has made the writing of this book possible.

SPECIAL ACKNOWLEDGMENTS

It takes a village to raise up and mentor a new writer. A special thanks to Nancy Lovell of Lovell-Fairchild Communications, to Chuck Colson and to my editors Becky English and Geoff Stone, whose advice, encouragement and mentoring have only made this book better. Others include Alton Gansky and Yvonne Lehman of the Blue Ridge Christian Writer's Conference, Linda Gilden of Class Services, Vonda Skelton and Edie Melson of the Christan Writer's Den, Leonard Goss, Steve Barclift, Daniel Johnson, Donna Savage and David Webb.

Thanks to all the folks at CLC Publications—Dave Fessenden, Dave Almack and Becky English—who have stood behind me and my God-given story.

Thanks also to Sydney Swails Brant Photography of North Charleston, South Carolina, for the author photo as well as the recent Brant, Montgomery and Dent family pictures.

CONTENTS

FOREWORD

Did you pick up this book to read the exciting story of a major political figure who survived with honor the Nixon debacle? If so, you won't be disappointed. This inside story of the Nixon years—told here for the first time—is very compelling. But you will find so much more.

It's hard to tell which is more fascinating—Harry Dent, the pre-conversion, hard-driving political activist (until age forty-eight) or his equally hard-driving post-conversion life. Instead of Washington impact, international impact; instead of working as a time-bound visionary, driving hard for eternal impact upon the woes of time. The story is fascinating, well told, with intrigue or suspense on almost every page.

Will you agree with all his choices? Probably not. Neither did he! For example, to enjoy this story you don't have to agree with Harry Dent's strongly expressed political views nor those of his "Sassy Pooh," as he called his beloved daughter. Nor must you agree with his approach to rescuing his second love—Romania. But his passionate love glows incandescently—for America, then for God.

Surely you'll be drawn to join the dance of father and daughter, as Ginny Dent Brant puts it, throughout the book. For in truth, this is two biographies, not one—the stories of a brilliant father and a gifted daughter intertwined throughout.

You'll feel the heartbeat of a teen experiencing the glory and grief inside the White House. A beauty queen? Yes, but more— a spiritual catalyst for the transformation of a very successful politicians' politician. *Time* magazine called Harry Dent "the architect of the Southern Republican revolution." Pre-Dent, the South was pervasively Democratic; post-Dent, Republican.

Here, intertwined with her own fascinating story, Ginny Brant, a proven leader in her own right, tells the story of a famous father whom she admired and loved deeply, and whom she wooed into a living relationship with Jesus Christ. It was a transformation that changed a political mover and shaker into a power for God's kingdom. And she tells her own story of pain and triumph, transformation and purpose with equal skill and passion.

Finding True Freedom is hard to put down, not only because of new revelations of high level intrigue and even Higher Level purpose and power, but because it is compellingly told.

Robertson McQuilkin
Author and President Emeritus
Columbia International University

WATERGATE— MORE THAN A FANCY HOTEL

Every divorce has three sides: his, hers and the truth. The great national divorce of 1974—the year a nation and its president cited irreconcilable differences and went separate ways—probably has as many stories, as many aspects and as many truths as people affected by it.

I was one of the children in that divorce, part of the collateral damage. I was seventeen years old when Richard Nixon's second term was underway. The nightmare for my family began on a late afternoon in March 1973, when Sam Donaldson of *ABC World News Tonight*, prominent and unassailable, broke the scoop that my father, Harry S. Dent, and Charles Colson had masterminded the Watergate break-in. When the formidable nightly news makes its report, what recourse does it leave the accused? For four weeks the word of a newscaster with a bad source hung on our family like a fitted noose.

My story is about those four weeks after "he did it" and about the stressful string of months between a back-page mention of a hotel break-in and a United States president relinquishing his post in front of the entire world. But the story doesn't stop there. While I certainly provide a daughter's-eye-view of the political break-up that rocked the world and the public humiliation that rocked many families, Watergate was a prelude to a greater story, a story of redemption—a Watergate in microcosm, if you will. My father, one of only two White House insiders to avoid prison for the Watergate affair, came at last to personal judgment. It is a story for which I had a front-row seat. In fact, my dad and I went through it together.

When Dad died in 2007, a couple of leading papers (the *Washington Post*, for one) compressed the summary of his life into the "Southern Strategy" (more about that later) and a foot-note to the shame of Watergate. That's fine, for that's what the writers knew. But after Watergate ended, Harry Dent lived an-other thirty-three years. It was another whole lifetime, and very different from the first one, at that.

What the obituaries missed is that for those involved, the Watergate disaster did not end with a whimper—nor with a president's shame or the handing out of twenty-five prison sen-tences. Dad's next chapter was anything but the post-White House cliché of golf games, federal pensions and the speakers' circuit.

Between 1954 and 1980, Harry Dent served a US sena-tor and three presidents, and he prepared his kids for similar achievements. He entered politics, and later practiced law, be-cause he genuinely believed these endeavors would help secure essential freedoms for humankind. While Watergate staggered us all, Dad's real undoing came when I bucked the plans he had for my life. But with great irony, Harry Dent, once a denizen of 1600 Pennsylvania Avenue, ultimately left his law practice to follow my footsteps and become everything he had always vehemently opposed. In his post-Watergate chapter, Harry Dent tried to block my path toward true freedom as though my life depended on it. Finally, he took the path himself, because he discovered his own desperate need for it.

Harry S. Dent's life amounted to far more than a so-called Southern Strategy and national politics. He would end his life in the opposite position from that of his early days. Yet his life was more blessed and fulfilled than he ever dreamed it would be. It was in the direction of true freedom.

*   *   *   *   *

When I was a junior in high school in Washington DC, life was simple and the social lines were clear. My father worked in the White House, where good men led the nation that led the world. The Watergate was a modern, upscale, crescent-shaped hotel-condominium and office complex on the Potomac; it had multiple swimming pools and a spectacular view of the Kennedy Center. I used to hang out there, sunbathing and swimming with my friend Sheila Meeder Weber. It was a place of prestige and class that would later become global shorthand for political conspiracy and a constant specter to my family.

My world was populated with the families of Dad's world. I can still picture fun with Kiki Kleindienst (daughter of Nixon's attorney general) as well as visits to the Ehrlichman home and snow-skiing trips with their kids. Tom Ehrlichman (son of Nixon's chief domestic advisor) and I tutored inner-city students together as part of a Langley High School project. My sister Dolly and I helped Julie Nixon (President Nixon's daughter) set up a presidential banquet at the Washington Hilton (where President Reagan was later shot in 1981).

We were all "the president's kids," escorting cabinet members onstage and taking in James Taylor and Carol King at the Kennedy Center from the president's box. We were the junior inner circle, rolling Easter eggs on the White House lawn and hanging ornaments for West Wing Christmas parties.

By the time I was seventeen, the break-in that forever grafted the words "president" and "scandal" was sprouting leaks and bugs and indictments all over the capital. Vietnam War protests and space exploration were in the headlines. *Hair* appeared on Broadway and *The Godfather* was showing at theaters. Three national networks owned the airwaves, and those airwaves owned our lives. Evening newscasts showed my dad's associates not in West Wing conversations or at high-level events but as defendants sinking in loose mud, pulling my father down with them. Every radio broadcast, every newspaper or newscaster, everywhere two or more journalists were gathered was cause for fear—my father, Nixon's other aides and all our families lived in the tightening vise of words like "obstruction of justice," "conspiracy" or "perjury."

And the thing was, most of the words were right on the money. At the highest levels of the US government, powerful egos had outstripped wisdom and common sense. The Watergate scandal was full of lies and pride and secrets. The scandal reached the highest levels and became a roll call of national embarrassment: Attorney General John Mitchell, Attorney General Richard Kleindienst, Commerce Secretary Maurice Stans, White House Chief of Staff Bob Haldeman, Chief Domestic Advisor John Ehrlichman, Special Counsel Chuck Colson, Special Assistant Jeb Magruder, Counsel John Dean and Special Counsel Egil Krogh.

Watergate haunted us for years. It was a darkness that was hard to explain. It was like an axe held over us, ready to execute disgrace on my family. If only I could dust off the years and recapture the sixteen-year-old innocence of my childlike days—before a national debacle expanded dictionaries with terms like "plumber" and "deep throat," amid others. Those were the days in which the men in my father's world were still the giants in mine.

The biggest blow to me, and the nation, was on August 9, 1974, when Richard Nixon became the first US president to leave his post before his term officially ended. Watching it on TV, I stood and wept. My father's political hero, along with his wife whom I adored, crossed the White House back lawn to a waiting helicopter while an unwieldy assembly of media documented the whole disgraceful exit.

That fateful day I was waiting tables and lying low at the Caliboque Café in Sea Pines on Hilton Head Island. Up to that point I had said almost nothing to anyone about my father or my family's link to the stories on the evening news. Most of my fellow waiters couldn't have identified Walter Cronkite or David Brinkley in a lineup. Only my manager knew my connection to the history being made. While my feet sprouted roots in front of the TV over the bar, I began to cry. Tears pooled under my chin and splattered on the table. I quickly wiped them up, hoping no one would notice.

My manager noticed. "Take a couple minutes," he said, as he covered my tables for me. As the helicopter rose and headed off, I grabbed ice tea and water pitchers to head back to the diners. But first I stepped into an empty banquet room and sobbed. This was more than devastation. We had given our hearts and souls to this administration. It was just too hard to believe.

Two years earlier, the Dents had been on top of the world. Now, at eighteen years old, I was stripped of all my heroes. A president was leaving office, a nation was limping, and the days ahead were about to test more than the guilty.

PART ONE

Fighting for Freedom

1

CHILDHOOD IN TWO CAPITALS

Not many kids are able to grow up in a near-perfect environ-ment, but I was one them. My mom and dad had a devout love for each other. They met at a high-school dance in St. Mat-thews. My mother was just fourteen years old when my dad swept her off her feet, literally, to win the dance contest that night. My father always proclaimed, "I've been dancing to her tune ever since."

My parents also had an undying devotion for their four chil-dren. I grew up with an older brother and sister to look up to and a younger brother to love and coddle. I lived in a whole-some, close-knit neighborhood where everyone celebrated holi-days and community events together. I attended school in one of the top public school systems in the country, in Fairfax County, and my family attended Plymouth Haven Baptist Church. To top it off, I grew up in the nation's capital, which when I was a little girl was the most revered and possibly the most beautiful city in the world. It doesn't get much better than that.

Yes, I had a wonderful, blessed and well-rounded childhood. Now, as an adult and an elementary school counselor, I know how good I had it. Yes, I had it all! I had every resource one needs to be successful. Though money cannot buy them, the simple things in life are usually the most valuable.

Childhood Innocence

In the late fifties Washington DC was a wonderful place to raise a family. We were always going to patriotic parades and celebrations. My father was simply one of those God-and-country men who lived and breathed his philosophy. The cost of living was reasonable, and the traffic was bearable. I grew up around many South Carolina people who were living in the DC area and working for Senator Strom Thurmond, as my dad was. I have fond memories of cookouts with the families on his staff. The senator had a knack for hiring some of the most wonderful people, and most of them have remained friends of mine to this day.

Senator Thurmond's DC office was in the Senate Office Building. It had tall ceilings, dark wood-stained doors and marble accents. My dad worked many long hours in that building as an administrative assistant, helping to run the senator's office. It was demanding to work on the staff of US Senator Strom Thurmond. Dad also went to law school at night and studied hard on the weekends. That wasn't easy to do with three children vying for his time and attention, but my father could study with a book in one hand and three kids on his lap. My dad would do anything for his children. But I learned early in life that if you wanted to spend time with him, you had to go where he was.

On Saturdays I would sometimes go into the office with my father. The senator was usually in his office, as well, and he'd move to another desk so I could watch my cartoons on his television set. He'd bring me bottled water and juices, carrots, celery and fruit. "Don't eat too much junk food" and "Drink lots of clean water," he would always say. Senator Thurmond was always way ahead of his time. When I was bored with cartoons, he would find something for me to do, whether it was stuffing envelopes or stamping things. My father and the senator had something in common—they both loved to spoil children.

My favorite part of the Senate Building was the underground trolley car going to the Capitol. We would always take a ride, sometimes over and over again. Running errands to the Capitol was the highlight of my day. I loved all the stone statues and the well-known Capitol Rotunda. And of course, it meant a ride on the trolley car. The senator always gently scolded me for not wanting to walk, but being the softy that he was, he would always give in for me. While I certainly was Daddy's girl, sometimes I guess you could say that I was the senator's girl.

At lunchtime, Dad would take me downstairs to the Senate cafeteria, and I would always get the same thing—a hamburger with pickles on top, french fries and milk. Guess who talked me into getting the milk? "Milk builds strong bones and teeth," the senator would always say. I used to ask for a handful of pickles to make up for the fries—just to keep the senator off my back. He was my first living example of a health nut.

While I was eating hamburgers with pickles, my father and Senator Thurmond were out to save the world. I was born in 1955, the year after Strom Thurmond was first elected to the United States Senate from South Carolina. In 1957 Senator Thurmond became famous for his more-than-twenty-four-hour filibuster, the longest in congressional history. Some say he was standing for states' rights; some say he was against civil rights legislation; and some saw it as nothing more than an impressive display of bladder control. It was my father who pushed the pitcher of water away, disappointing other senators who were hoping a drink of water would send him running to relieve himself.

It was in 1954 that the Supreme Court of the United States declared "separate, but equal" unconstitutional in the Brown versus the Board of Education case. Then, during the first year of my life, the United States adopted "In God We Trust" as our national motto. You might say I was born in the best of times. Still a baby, I had no idea how these things would one day affect my life.

Since both of my grandfathers passed away before I was born, Senator Thurmond was like a grandfather to me. He treated all the office staff children as his own. He would bring us special gifts when he returned from trips. My jewelry box still contains the brooch he brought me from Portugal. His wife, Jean, was also very kind. She was a gentle woman. She worked tirelessly for the senator and his causes, as did my dad. People later said that my father and Jean Thurmond became like siblings because of the long hours they shared promoting the senator and his work.

I can remember how afraid I was when I saw Mrs. Thurmond's shaved head after her treatment for brain cancer. It was the first time I'd heard the word "cancer." She was always so kind—and then she was gone. At her funeral in June of 1960, when I was only five years old, my father heard grief-stricken Senator Thurmond say to Lyndon Johnson, "I hope you are the next president of the United States."[1] In time, however, those feelings would change.

After Jean's death the senator buried himself in his work. He also spent more time at our home in Alexandria. I remember the time he took my siblings and me sledding. He lay down on the sled, and the three of us piled on top. Playing with the senator was more fun than playing with other grown-ups. He actually had as much energy as we had, and that was saying a lot!

There were so many good people in my life when I was growing up that I assumed all people were good. I was so innocent. I thought that everyone loved God and wanted to serve Him. That all doctors went into medicine to help heal others. That all ministers wanted to serve God and His creation. That all politicians and government leaders were honorable and called to serve the public trust. And that all families had two parents, like I did. I was naïve, but it was great while it lasted.

A bit of my naiveté died the day President John F. Kennedy was assassinated in 1963. I was in the third grade, and we got out of school early. I walked home in shock with tears in my eyes. I was glued to the TV, and I had a hard time sleeping that night. My father took me to the Rotunda to view the presidential casket, and we stood on the side of the road as the horse-drawn caisson went by on its way to Arlington Cemetery. Later my dad took us all to see the eternal flame above the president's grave. In looking back I think that horrible incident was the first picture of violence I had seen on TV. I mourned, and the country mourned. A nation was struck with grief.

It was also in the third grade that I made a very important decision in my life. I decided to be baptized. It was a big decision for an eight-year-old little girl. It was even more difficult for me because I was extremely shy. I was so shy that if I saw someone I knew walking down the street, I would simply lower my head because I was too afraid to say hello. I was an intense introvert. Psychologists might even say that I had low self-esteem. I wasn't super intelligent like my older brother Harry Jr. (we call him Hank). Neither was I coordinated and athletically inclined like my older sister Dolly. And I didn't have the gregarious personality of my younger brother Jack, who could win anyone over. Quite honestly, I wasn't good at any particular thing.

I was young when I started first grade at five years old, and I struggled to learn to read. Moreover, I stuttered until I was in third grade. Although my parents supported me in whatever I did, I know they were more concerned about me than they were about my siblings. It took every bit of nerve I had to walk down the church aisle and get baptized in front of the whole congregation. My older brother and sister were baptized with me. From that point on, I tried to live my life as the Bible said and to follow every rule. Yet something was missing.

My Dad, the Freedom Fighter

My friends admired the dolls my father brought me from his travels overseas. He used them to teach me about how my life in the US was different from the rest of the world. I remember that he brought me dolls from Iran and Iraq.

"Dad, why are their faces covered?" I asked.

"It's just part of their religion. They simply don't have the freedoms that we have here," he responded.

I placed them on my shelf of dolls that my father had brought me from the lands across the sea, and they always stood out. The Iraq doll draped in black from her head to her toes always commanded the most attention.

The joy and the price of freedom were very important to my father. As a matter of fact, before my father worked for the senator, he had volunteered to serve in the Korean War for the cause of freedom. He had lost his two older brothers in World War II, and another brother had been seriously injured. From his early years he had been a freedom fighter. His family had paid the ultimate price for freedom. They were like the folks in the movie *Saving Private Ryan*. When a military officer discovered my father was from a family who had already sacrificed so much for the cause of freedom, he removed him from the front lines. But my father continued to serve in the National Guard for many years. He traveled on missions with the Guard and to faraway lands with Senator Thurmond.

While I was arranging my doll collection and soaking up all that the great capital city had to offer, my father and Senator Thurmond were working on the so-called Southern Strategy. "Southern Strategy" is the term used for any political tactic to win over Southern votes in a national election. John F. Kennedy was the first to use it when he was running for president in 1960. He selected a Southerner, Lyndon Baines Johnson, as his running mate, promised to protect the South's textile industry from low-cost imports and made a sympathy call to Martin Luther King Jr. during his imprisonment in an Atlanta jail.[2] The aim of the Southern Strategy wasn't to rule the country or ruin the opposition but simply to have the South treated like any other part the US.

Having been marginalized politically since the end of the Civil War, in the 1960s the South needed to change two things in order to get back to national prominence. The first thing they needed was a strong second-party option. For many years Southerners had voted Democrat because that was what their daddies did; even when the Democrats didn't represent the people's views, Southerners still voted the party line. The second important change they needed was to find a peaceful and honorable resolution of their racial problems. This would take time.[3]

It was in the summer of 1964 that my dad and his beloved friend and cohort, Fred Buzhardt Jr., worked to convince Senator Thurmond to switch to the Republican Party and fight for Barry Goldwater (a.k.a. "Mr. Conservative"), the Republican Party's nominee for the upcoming elections. Both Fred and my dad, who worked together writing Thurmond's speeches, arranging his schedule and giving advice, had plenty of pull with the senator. They pointed out to him the liberal voting record of Democratic nominee Lyndon Baines Johnson following John F. Kennedy's assassination. But it was Johnson's selection of ultra-liberal Hubert Humphrey as his running mate in 1964 that made Thurmond agree to switch parties and transfer his loyalties.

On September 16, 1964, Thurmond told the people of South Carolina and the South, "To my friends who have conscientiously advised me against this step because of a sincere belief that I could best serve the country by following a course to keep myself in office, I can only say that I fully realize the political risk involved in this step; I could go down into oblivion. But in the final analysis, I can only follow the course that in my heart and conscience I believe to be in the best interest of our state, our country, and the freedom of our people. I have chosen this course because I cannot consider any risks in a cause which I am convinced is right."[4]

My dad, the senator and Fred Buzhardt worked relentlessly for Goldwater all over the South. The "Thurmond Speaks for Goldwater Campaign" was done without any assistance from the Goldwater camp. My father left his position in Thurmond's Capitol office to operate the special campaign. He had to take a pay cut, and we had to move to Columbia, South Carolina, which sent me into a tailspin. I'll never forget the day my father came home from work and informed us that we were moving so that he could take a new job. It was the fall of 1964, during my fifth grade year. He said he was leaving his post as head of Thurmond's office to help Senator Goldwater in his run for the presidency.

Doesn't anyone consider talking to the children first? We'd spent many summers vacationing at Folly Beach in South Carolina. We had often visited family and relatives in St. Matthews, including Bet and Sue, two fine black ladies who had helped raise my dad while his mother ran the family business. But in my mind, South Carolina was a place we only visited. How could we live there? How could Dad make me give up everything I loved? I was devastated.

We sold most of our belongings and packed up with only a week's notice. I said goodbye to my fifth-grade teacher, my best friend from kindergarten, Carol Connor Willingham, and my other friends. I rode in the U-Haul truck with my dad and cried the whole way. Moving wasn't easy for any of us kids, but it was most difficult for me because I was so shy, and it took me much longer to adjust to new places. I know it broke my father's heart to see the pain his children were going through—especially me. I was Daddy's little girl. He did everything he could to try to make it up to all of us.

Although Goldwater won most of the South, he lost overwhelmingly throughout the nation. Goldwater supporters knew that the South in and of itself wasn't enough to win a presidential election. Quite honestly, some people believed that Goldwater never expected to win. But his victory in the South germinated the seed in the Republican Southern Strategy which had begun to sprout and grow. After the presidential election of 1964, Goldwater fever would set the stage for the rise and development of a competitive two-party system.

These new Republicans were concerned with saving America from the leftward gallop of the Democrat donkey. They stood

for individual freedom versus government control, free enterprise versus the trend toward socialism, and a strong national
defense against the formidable enemy of our liberty—Communism.[5]

Although Senator Thurmond won the 1964 Senate election
and held his valuable seat, he was one of only two conservative
Republicans in that governing body. In the end, by doing what
he felt was right in switching parties, Thurmond had enhanced
his own political prestige rather than detracted from it. By 1968
Republicans had six conservatives in the Senate and twenty-nine
in the House. Republicans were beginning to say, "We're gonna
win from the court house to the White House!"[6]

When South Carolina Republicans were looking for a leader
in 1965, my father was the likely candidate. He actually gave up
the salary and benefits from his job with Senator Thurmond and
took this new position, without pay, as chairman of the South
Carolina GOP. The previous chairmen had all been independently wealthy—but not my dad. My father began to practice
law on the side to generate revenue, and my mother went back
to work for the first time since my brother Harry Jr. had been
born to help produce a stable income and provide health benefits. This was part of the price my parents paid to serve. What
my father did in his career was never about money. It was all
about serving a purpose. And that purpose always had to do
with freedom.

My dad's job as chairman of the Republican Party in South
Carolina kept him quite busy and on the road frequently. As I
mentioned earlier, I learned at an early age that if you wanted
to be a part of my dad's life, you had to go where he went. He
enjoyed taking us with him all over South Carolina to support
the Republican candidates running for office. On one such trip
the single-engine airplane we were in had to make an emergency
landing in a field. My mother was beside herself that night. I can
still remember the fear in her voice when she said, "No more
single-engine planes for my babies!" She laid down the law in

our household, and my father respected her wishes. Hence the saying, "When Betty Francis talks, Harry listens."

There was nowhere I would rather have been than with my dad. I even spent Saturdays at the Republican Party headquarters on Harden Street just like I had done at the Capitol in DC. Traveling with my father to stump meetings and political debates is what caused me to start calling him Harry instead of Daddy. When you're a child in a room filled with men who are all talking politics, no one responds when you say "Daddy." They always just kept on talking, since all of them were daddies. Calling my father Harry had nothing to do with disrespect. There was no one I loved or respected more than him.

All my father's hard work paid off. Bob McAlister, a friend and co-worker of my dad's, would later say that Harry Dent had been Strom Thurmond's alter ego. He averred that my father had engineered Thurmond's party switch in 1964 and laid the foundation for the GOP takeover in South Carolina. Van Hipp Jr., now chief executive officer of DC-based consulting firm American Defense International, relayed the same sentiment when he exclaimed that it was my father who built the modern-day Republican Party in South Carolina and in the rest of the South. Senate Minority Leader Mitch McConnell remarked several years ago that "Harry Dent was the single person most responsible for building the Republican Party in the South, and he paved the way for guys like me to get elected."[7]

My First Encounter with the Nixons

In those days in Columbia, I was able to walk to school. One day, on my way home, I found my precious dog Peppy lying in the street. He'd been hit by a car, and his body was stiff. I threw a blanket over him to protect my little brother from seeing the tragic sight. At the very time I found him, my parents were on an airplane with former Vice President Richard Nixon. Those were the years when Nixon was traveling through the South, drumming up support for the Republican presidential nomination. I contacted my father's secretary, and she sent Hal and Betty Byrd, friends of the family, over to help us handle the situation. They performed a short funeral service in our backyard and helped us bury Peppy. My father's secretary must have told my father about the tragedy while they were on their flight with the Nixons. My parents were sorry they couldn't be with us, but they returned home as soon as possible to console us.

A few days after the accident, the doorbell rang. I opened the door only to be run over and vigorously licked by a hyperactive, curly-haired dog. "Vice President and Mrs. Nixon send their sympathies," the man said.

My brother and I were thrilled with the gift, and we decided to name the dog "Richard." We ended up needing a fence to contain this energetic, wire-haired pet, because whenever he escaped, he always ended up harassing one of our Democrat neighbors. It was as if he knew we were Republicans. The next day an article appeared in the paper with my brother Jack and our new dog, Richard.

It took me two years to adjust to my new life in South Carolina, but the moved turned out okay. In time, I eventually grew to love Columbia, and I relented of my anger toward my father. I knew he had an important job and that he only wanted what was best for us. Even though this move had been a difficult and painful time for me, I was still a daddy's girl.

2

Coming Into Our Own

It took several years for me to call Columbia my hometown. As a matter of fact, I began to grow quite attached to that old cotton town. The longer you live somewhere, the more you learn to love it. By 1967 I had made many friends. My mother enrolled me in a basic modeling class, which helped me get over my fear of people. I was in the seventh grade, and I really began to blossom. I ran for student council and won. At the end of eighth grade, I tried out for cheerleading with the help of my older sister, Dolly (the naturally coordinated one). She helped me with my jumps and dance steps. All the extra coaching must have helped. They announced the new cheerleaders in an assembly program; I waited anxiously as each name was called. My name was the last one.

Later that school year, I was tapped to be in a sorority called *Les Friponnes*, which gave me a close group of friends. At the end of ninth grade, I was named to May Court. Modeling became a very important part of my life. After school I modeled in fashion shows and acted in commercials. I was beginning to find my niche.

The Southern Strategy Takes Root

My whole world began gradually to change in Columbia, and things began to make sense. I was finally fitting in and coming into my own. While things were coming together for me, my father was bringing Southern Republicans into their own. He was helping to maneuver the South to the forefront in politics and eventually into the White House. After my dad had been chairman of the South Carolina Republican Party for only a year, the 1966 elections in South Carolina showed a gain for the new Republicans—they went from having a single state legislator to twenty-three, as well as many more local offices. The seeds of the Southern Strategy were continuing to bear fruit. Nationally, the Republican Party picked up forty-seven seats in the House and four in the Senate.

The Southern Strategy was an effort of loyal Southern politicians like Senator Thurmond and my dad—men who could no longer support the National Democratic Party, which had gradually moved too far to the left for them. Since just before the beginning of the twentieth century, Southern politicians had been treated like second-class citizens. Certain politicians with strong convictions wanted the region once again to have a voice in the direction our country was taking.

The Democrats didn't like these changing opinions within their ranks. When the Democratic Party started giving the impression that they would whip the already beaten-down South back into line, two prominent Southern politicians defected to the Republicans—Senator Strom Thurmond and Governor George Wallace of Alabama. Contrary to a popular view fostered by liberals, only Wallace's defection was substantially based on race. Wallace vowed in his 1963 inauguration speech, "Segregation now, segregation tomorrow and segregation forever." Later that year Governor Wallace rose to national attention when he "stood at the schoolhouse door" to oppose two young black students from entering the University of Alabama. It was Wallace who called for "law and order" as an anti-black agenda.[1] Thurmond's defection, on the other hand, clearly stemmed from his opposition to big government, excessive spending, national interest and soft foreign policy.

Although Thurmond had filibustered over the Civil Rights Act of 1957 in an effort to maintain segregation (a record twenty-four hours and eighteen minutes), he later moderated his position and began to see that things needed to change in the South. Thurmond and other Southerners like my dad had supported segregation in their early days simply because it was the Southern way of life. As they grew politically and morally, so did their recognition of the rights of all Americans, black or white, and their determination to include them.

The real reason for the Southern Strategy was to return America to conservative policies at the national level so the free enterprise system could be preserved and individual freedoms protected. If the purpose of the Southern Strategy had been to turn back the clock to pre-May 17, 1954 (the Supreme Court desegregation decision), its supporters would have gone with Wallace. They clearly did not.[2] Senator Thurmond and my father both strongly felt this nation must keep a check on the size and control of the federal government if we were going to continue to live in the land of the free and the home of the brave—and they supported candidates who felt the same.

Three men would step up to the plate in a run for the Republican nomination for president in 1968: Ronald Reagan, Nelson Rockefeller and Richard Nixon. Nixon, already vice president, made clear to my dad his intention to seek the presidency. He felt that his chief roadblock would be George Wallace, who intended to run as an independent. Nixon knew he needed Southerners to get his party's nomination, but he wasn't initially planning on courting the South in a national election. But one night, after drumming up support in South Carolina, his plane was running late. While he waited for the plane, my father was able to convince him that the Southern Strategy was important.

Ronald Reagan was also a favorite to many in South Carolina with his undeniable charisma, good looks and conservative ideology. In 1967 he had come to South Carolina to raise funds in order to help retire $40,000 of Republican debt left over from the 1966 elections. The debt accrued during the three-year peri-od that my father had worked as the chairman of the Republican Party. My father had taken the job without pay, since money was scarce; the party certainly had no way to pay off the debt. My dad had always admired Reagan, but after Reagan's fundraising campaign, Dad loved him even more for getting his name off that debt! Still, because of Reagan's lack of experience in national and international affairs, my father personally concluded that the time was right not for him but for Richard Nixon.

Nixon had always been clear about his support of the Su-preme Court's ruling which had overturned the old separate-but-equal system of education for blacks and whites. He was, however, opposed to forced busing of students as a means of achieving racial balance—forcing a mix of races in the schools just to prove that desegregation was occurring. Nixon favored "civil rights" as opposed to "civil wrongs."

Senator Thurmond, too, felt that Nixon was the best candi-date for the party and for the cause of freedom. Thurmond felt Nixon's civil rights position was the most satisfactory of the can-didates. My dad and the senator worked hard to make sure Nix-on got the Republican Party's nomination in Miami in 1968. It was a tough race between Reagan and Nixon, but Nixon ended up winning. After his acceptance speech, Nixon held a meet-ing in his suite to help select the vice presidential candidate. My father and Senator Thurmond plugged for Reagan. But after receiving a room full of feedback and trying to appease every-one, Nixon chose Governor Spiro Agnew from Maryland. Even though their first choice had been Reagan, Senator Thurmond and my father gave a thumbs-up on Agnew.

My dad and the senator spent the next few months trying to stop George Wallace, who ran as an independent, from taking conservative votes and handing the presidency to the Democrat-ic candidate, former Vice President Hubert Humphrey. As usu-al, Dad's multiple jobs kept him busy. He practiced law to earn a living, ran the Republican Party in South Carolina and worked on Nixon's presidential bid. Needless to say, he was never home.

From Southern Strategist to Presidential Aide

Senator Thurmond and my father shifted from king savers to kingmakers when Nixon emerged the victor in the cliff-hanging presidential race. In the end, Nixon won with 38 percent of the vote, Wallace and Humphrey fighting for second. My father was heralded by the *New York Times* as the Southern strategist who helped Richard Nixon carry the South in the 1968 presidential election.

Within thirty days of the election, my father was installed in New York City for about two months as a deputy counsel during the transition period. His subsequent position with the Nixon administration proved that deals had been made with the Southern GOP and that there was indeed a Nixon Southern Strategy. The Nixon administration tried to downplay my father's appointment, but the *New York Times* caught the gist, and their reporter, John Apple, called it a "small quid for a big quo."[3]

After Nixon won, my father came home excited to tell us he had been asked to go to Washington to be one of the president's men. Instead of congratulating him, my sister, my mother and I sat down and cried. "How can you do this to us?" we lamented. He thought we'd be excited for him, but he didn't get the response he had hoped for. With three kids in high school all complaining, he decided that he would commute to Washington and leave the five of us in Columbia where we were safe and happy. It isn't that we weren't supportive and excited for him; we just didn't want to move.

Dad moved into his new office in the Executive Office Building on January 21, 1969. Our entire family was decked out for the occasion. It was the first of many inaugurations and balls that we attended. Inaugural balls aren't what people might think. In those days you waited for hours, packed into a crowded room, to catch a glimpse of the president and his first lady. If you tried to dance, you merely got your feet stepped on. There wasn't enough room.

We would find that politics can sometimes be like those balls, with everyone climbing over each other just for a chance to reach the top. Within six months Nixon elevated my father's position by moving him to the East Wing of the White House. Later his office would be moved back to the Executive Office Building—a demotion that our family would eventually celebrate.

In my father's first White House meeting, H.R. Haldeman told the entire staff that memos would be the principal means of communication with top men at the White House and the president. The aides were told to make their memos concise and clear, and to leave nothing to the imagination since everything was covered by executive privilege. Executive privilege is defined as "the right of the president to maintain the secrecy of his communications with his White House aides." These words gave all the aides a sense of security—a security that would one day be ripped away with one stroke of a judge's pen.

The Senator Takes a Bride

During the presidential election, Senator Thurmond postponed his wedding plans with a very young Nancy Janice Moore (Miss South Carolina 1966) at the request of my father and Fred Buzhardt. My father and Buzhardt were both afraid the relationship would ruin him politically.

As soon as the election was over, though, Senator Thurmond had held off as long as he could. He was ready to marry his young bride. Again, my father and Fred tried to coax him out of marrying Nancy, afraid that their age difference might ruin Thurmond's political career. They even got the senator's permission to speak to Nancy and try to talk her out of it. Neither of them would budge on their plans, so my father advised a small wedding with no media attention. In December of 1968, much to his chagrin, they planned a large wedding, complete with media coverage, in Aiken, South Carolina. They held the reception at the home of the president of the University of South Carolina and had over fifteen hundred guests in attendance.

I was one of the guests at that wedding reception of Senator and Nancy Thurmond. I leaned over to my dad and commented on their age difference: "Twenty-two times three equals sixty-six."

My father politely told me, "I've already mentioned that, and don't bring it up again." I certainly thought the senator was far too old for his bride. However, I admired him so much that I learned to accept the respect and love that he and his wife had for each other. My father had tried everything he could to stop what he thought was the greatest mistake of the senator's life. Four children later, however, Nancy and the senator were still in love, and Thurmond's popularity never waned. My father was proven wrong.

Working toward Desegregation

One of the first things Nixon did in office was to order the schools in the South to desegregate. So just before my second year of high school in Columbia, in the fall of 1970, my sister and I were zoned to a new school. Now here I was, heading into my sophomore year and having to leave my friends behind again. For me, it was a very sad time. Instead of going to A.C. Flora, we attended our cross-town rival, Dreher High School. It appeared that once again my whole life was to change overnight. My friends and I planned one last slumber party together, and we all cried as if our world was coming to an end.

It seemed so unfair. I was a typical teenager who thought life was supposed to be all about me. Little did I know that I was just part of the great desegregation experiment—the plan to end the racial segregation that had plagued the South for years. There was nothing my sister and I could do about the heartbreaking change of schools.

Fortunately, a few of my friends were sent to Dreher too. I was too young then to know that God uses all the circumstances in our lives for our good. But my sister and I were determined to make the best out of this situation.

As upset as we were about the transition, we were too naïve to figure out that my father was the man behind the man who was doing this. My father, of all Nixon's appointees, was one of the main ones advising him to desegregate the South, starting with education. And, he encouraged, locals should be allowed to control the process as much as possible. If we had known how influential our dad was in desegregating our schools, we might have raised a fuss.

My father worked busily behind the scenes to make sure everything went smoothly. He was wiser than most and knew that desegregation would only work if the Southern people went along with the plan. The guidelines had to be administered with the end result of winning compliance and cooperation as opposed to force. The Kennedy and Johnson administrations had tried to use force, threats, retaliation and defunding. Retaliation and force never work. But local control allows representatives of all affected parties to come up with practical solutions, communicating and selling them to their people. Difficult problems are best worked out when everyone involved has ownership of the solution.

When several districts in the South were scheduled to have their funds terminated nine days after Nixon's inauguration due to unmet deadlines, my father convinced the president to grant a sixty-day reprieve. This reprieve gave the school district superintendents the right to hold onto the money while they negotiated with the Department of Health, Education and Welfare (HEW) desegregation teams. Within the sixty-day time period, five school districts negotiated successful plans to appease HEW. Later, when twenty-one school districts in South Carolina had problems with HEW, Nixon offered to personally negotiate the South Carolina cases, thus sending shockwaves through HEW.

Nixon's labor secretary, George Shultz, also helped with the desegregation of the South when a strike broke out at the Medical University of South Carolina over an equal-employment opportunity problem. If the dispute went unresolved, the Medical University would lose $12 million in federal aid. Sparks between the Nixon administration and the leftover HEW appointees from Lyndon Johnson's administration exacerbated the problem, since Johnson's approach to handling desegregation had been completely opposite Nixon's. George Shultz was a talented professor who was reasonable and persuasive. He helped the Nixon administration settle the strike without the university losing any federal funds. During this time Shultz and my father formed a lifelong friendship.

My father was the go-between for all parties involved with desegregation, including the black leaders. Black groups received as much, if not more, cooperation and time from my dad as the white groups did. Along with Bob Brown (a black assistant in the White House), my dad later helped the Nixon administration form a group of black administration appointees. On August 18, 1969, Simeon Booker, a black correspondent for *Ebony* and *Jet* magazines, wrote a letter to my dad expressing his opinions and gratitude for what he had done in his White House position:

> To be white and from South Carolina is reason enough for many Americans to become suspicious. Harry Dent is white. Harry Dent is from South Carolina. But in these troubled times, Harry Dent is the most effective White House aide for race relations.
>
> In reference to the Charleston strike, Dent, from behind the scenes, brought both sides together for negotiation. His involvement was considered an important asset toward the solution of the case.
>
> Harry Dent also asked that the widow of astronaut test pilot, Robert Lawrence, be invited to the Los Angeles state dinner for moon-flight heroes in 1968. NASA officials ruled against her being invited since her husband was only the first black test pilot in the space program. Dent disagreed, trying to give 25 million blacks recognition in the space project.

My father was always busy, but during desegregation he worked from 7:00 a.m. to 2:00 a.m. It was the price we paid for service to our country.

Blue Jeans in the White House

During my sophomore year, while my dad commuted and worked to promote freedom in America, I missed him terribly. Before that Christmas of 1970, one day late in the week, my good friend Jean Olson Cunningham and I decided to ride the overnight train to DC in our jeans and comfy sweatshirts. How we looked when we arrived the next morning must be left to imagination. My father met us with the White House limo—but instead of taking us to his apartment, as we had expected, he took us directly to the White House because an emergency meeting had been called.

"Don't worry," he said, "I'll hide you in my office in the East Wing and then take you to my apartment to change when the meeting is over." It was a normal day at the White House, and people were lined up anxiously waiting for the tours to begin. When they saw the limo go right through the crowds to the East Wing, they pointed and smiled as if celebrities were going to get out of the car. We stepped out of the limo in our beautiful jeans and sweatshirts, and someone exclaimed, "It must be Tricia and Julie!" (Nixon's daughters). Once they got a good look, though, people probably thought we were hired help.

I hid out in my father's office as long as I could, but White House meetings can go on forever. Eventually I had to use the ladies' room. Hoping no one would see me—and knowing my mother would kill me if they did—I sneaked out of my dad's office. On the way to the ladies' room, I ran into Pat Nixon! She spoke to me and I could barely say a word. I mean I really choked up. She was just as nice and down to earth as could be. I had been caught in the presidential mansion without makeup and in blue jeans by the First Lady. Barack Obama wasn't the first one to be casual in the White House!

Jean and I returned to Columbia on the train Sunday night. The next day at school, I was called out of class to receive a phone call from the White House. The principal allowed me to take the call in his office. It was Pat Nixon asking if I would like to read the Christmas story in the White House Christmas Service. I was speechless. Being shy, I declined the offer and volunteered my sister Dolly—but I guess my jeans and sweatshirt had made a good impression.

Nixon and Ceauşescu

To my father, there was no such thing as a good Communist; to Richard Nixon, however, some were better than others. Nixon made several trips to Romania, in which the Communists had seized power in 1947, to develop a relationship with Nicolae Ceauşescu. Ceauşescu was the leader of Romania from 1967 to 1989.

Nixon, in 1969, became the first American president after World War II to visit the country of Romania. Nixon was impressed that this little nation had been the first Warsaw Pact country to recognize West Germany; he also thought Romania forward moving to have joined the International Monetary Fund. Ceauşescu's role in helping to thaw relations between Peking and Washington further earned him the gratitude of Nixon.[4] The president saw him as a "man who could contribute to understanding and solving the world's most urgent global problems."[5] Margaret Thatcher was equally impressed with Ceauşescu, saying in 1978 that he was "willing to cooperate with other nations."[6]

A year after visiting Romania, Nixon invited Ceauşescu and his wife Elena to a special dinner in their honor at the White House. Even though he wasn't fond of any Communist leader being honored at the White House, my father attended the dinner, as he had many such affairs at the White House. He was puzzled by the whole affair, yet he knew Nixon was the master of foreign affairs and that this relationship with Ceauşescu was particularly significant to him.

Time would tell whether a Communist leader could really do right by his country. Only the future would reveal the significance this man and his actions would play in my father's life.

NIXON
AND
THE SOUTH

Nixon was a man who lived up to his promises. He loved the South from his days at Duke University Law School and he courted the South during his 1968 presidential election. Now was his time to deliver on what he had promised.

A man of conviction, Nixon was determined to end the dual system of education nationwide without violence. He never hid these convictions from his Southern supporters. Ending segregation and doing it successfully would take wise judgment and action.

Title VI was a part of the Civil Rights Act that required the cutting off of federal funding for local school districts that didn't comply with the desegregation law. Many people were critical of Nixon's administration, saying it was soft on desegregation when, instead of cutting off funds, it shifted to litigation procedures provided under that same act.[1] Previous administrations had tried cutting off funds to school districts in order to force them to comply with desegregation. Nixon favored litigation as a means of reconciliation rather than domination.

Before initiating the lawsuits, the president told southern school districts:

> Desegregation is required by law, and I am duty bound to enforce the law. You are in the best position to formulate and im-

plement your own desegregation plans. If you choose to do so in good faith and within Constitutional limits, we will accept your plans. If you fail to do so, the Federal Government will be required to devise a plan and require you to implement it by court action.[2]

These words indicated his willingness to rely on the "good faith" of the school districts. In addition, the president authorized $1.5 billion from Congress to help fund the desegregation process. He also named seven state advisory committees made up of private citizens of diverse ethnic backgrounds to help the Cabinet Committee on Education through the transition period. Nixon and my father wanted to achieve desegregation with the least possible disruption of children's education. They didn't want schoolchildren to be the victims.

Nixon, as mentioned, opposed compulsory busing out of normal geographic zones to achieve racial balance. You might say he took the "middle road" on desegregation. The most vocal critics of desegregation came from those who rode in limousines and sent their children to private schools, while my siblings and I and others like us, as part of the new experiment, were determined to play a part in making it work.

In looking back from where I stand as an educator today, I believe that the president and my father worked together to do the right thing. I know from experience that having neighborhood schools and local control help people develop a sense of belonging and community, which leads to better education. Teachers, parents and students work harder when neighborhood schools foster a sense of community.

It's common sense, and usually the federal government isn't known for using it. But in this area, Richard Nixon was ahead of his time in promoting strong communities. One of the seven advisory committees Nixon had set up, this one of South Carolinian business executives from both races, used an intensive media campaign with a message of "Keep Your Cool . . . Support Your School."

Many different groups and leaders got involved in supporting public education and desegregation. Rev. Billy Graham appealed to his followers, encouraging them to retain order during the process. He never allowed segregation at any of his crusades or events. It took courage for him to stand boldly against the status quo of his day. Even the media lent a helping hand by airing videos that Graham and other business leaders made to promote a "fair-minded chance." In this way the media was part of the solution rather than part of the problem.

No one was more pleased than my father at the way things progressed. He always thought about what would benefit everybody. He was a gifted peacemaker, whether in politics or at home. This is a skill I would eventually pick up from him. You can only be a peacemaker when you first see things from both sides and then know how the result will affect both sides. It's called "walking in another man's shoes."

The seven state advisory committees Nixon had appointed for the transition process were successful and effective. They brought a sense of ownership and compliance to what many feared would be a violent and difficult transition. No one said desegregation would be easy or without its problems. Although the political left was constantly criticizing that it wasn't done sooner and with force, time and history would prove that their recommendations had not been wise.

When speaking in Birmingham in May of 1971, President Nixon spoke about desegregation and praised the states below the Mason-Dixon Line for the progress they had made. "Today 38 percent of all black children in the South go to majority white schools, while only 28 percent of all black children in the North go to majority white schools. While there has been significant progress in the South, there has been no progress in the North in the past three years."[3]

Essie Mae Washington-Williams, in her 2005 book *Dear Senator*, wrote that America north of the Mason-Dixon Line wasn't the promised land for blacks. There she had to sit in the "colored balconies" of auditoriums; she and other blacks were not allowed to sit at the local soda fountain or swim in public pools. Witnessing the actual lynching of a black man in her Pennsylvania hometown marked the beginning of her black consciousness.[4]

Nixon himself felt a consciousness about the fact that things needed to change. He praised black and white leaders in the South for working together to bring about change—a change not all of them had agreed with, but one they cooperated with as law-abiding citizens.[5]

Desegregation had to be brought about—it was the right thing to do. In my father's eyes, President Nixon had delivered a slam dunk.

Civil Rights Gains

No one believed in Richard Nixon's vision for this country more than my father. Although the liberal media painted Nixon as being anti-black and anti-civil rights, my father knew they were wrong. My dad was the go-between for all the parties involved with desegregation, including the black leaders. Black groups received as much, if not more, cooperation and time from my dad.

In Nixon's first four years, he increased the civil rights enforcement budgets by 800 percent, appointed a record number of blacks to federal posts (an increase of 37 percent) and created the office of Minority Business Enterprise. Federal contracts to minority enterprises rose from $9 million to $153 million, small business loans to minorities increased over 1,000 percent, and US aid to black colleges more than doubled. More school integration was achieved in Nixon's four years than had been in the previous fifteen years since Brown versus the Board of Education.[6] And what was done was achieved without violence and without the force of troops. Worthy of mention is the fact that these victories were never reported by the liberal-leaning *Washington Post*.

Nixon appointed Leonard Garment to be his civil rights advocate in the White House, and Bob Brown, who worked closely with my dad, was installed as the top black aide in the administration. By 1972 Nixon had accomplished a record number of key black appointments, which exceeded those of the Kennedy and Johnson administrations combined.

In the end, Nixon's stand against forced busing was eventually validated by black columnist William Raspberry of the *Washington Post*, black superintendent Wilson Riles of California and famed sociologist James Coleman of the University of Chicago. Raspberry said, "It has been clear for some time that busing for purposes of integration was in its terminal stages. The question was whether Congress or the courts would administer the *coup de grâce*."[7] Dr. Riles pledged not to force busing on any school district as a means of desegregation.[8] Dr. Coleman wrote the initial report that instigated the mass busing movement, but in 1975 he reversed his support of busing as a means of achieving racial balance because, he said, it prompted "white flight."[9] *Time* magazine also weighed in with their opinion in its September 15, 1975, issue, which stated that "busing as a means of achieving racial imbalance in the schools may be the most unpopular institution imposed on Americans since Prohibition."[10]

My father gathered all the opinion polls and op-ed pieces he could find on busing. He was the ultimate researcher. He gathered data from all sides and used it to make good decisions. He was always keeping Nixon apprised of every bit of information he needed to know. The president had a gut feeling about busing from the start, and he stuck with it.

On January 9, 1971, my dad appealed to the South Carolina GOP to broaden their tent to appeal to all people. He wanted them to include both the white moderate and the new black electorate within its ranks. He encouraged other Republicans to extend acceptance as well as leadership to our black brothers and sisters. He called it the "wise thing to do."[11] My father was seeing that gradually the Southern GOP was becoming more and more integrated, as had the Southern Strategy. He saw, over time, a growing acceptance of desegregation.

My father encouraged Senator Strom Thurmond to hire a black staff member to represent the needs of the black community in South Carolina. Thurmond hired his first black legislative assistant, Thomas Moss, in 1971. In December of the same year, my father sent a memo urging the GOP to consider recruiting a black field person for every congressional district. He helped to coordinate a Bob Brown tribute dinner at the Washington Hilton with more than three thousand in attendance. He scheduled Sammy Davis Jr. as the Master of Ceremonies, and there was even an appearance at the event by President Nixon.

Textiles—the Lifeline of the South

The Southern Strategy had many facets. While desegregation was met with mixed feelings in the South, the Southern Strategy was about making it as painless as possible. It was about working at the local level, opposing big government and helping the South prosper political, socially and economically.

During Nixon's presidential campaign in 1968, my father had advised him to promise, ahead of his contenders, reasonable protection to the textile industry—the same thing John Kennedy had done ahead of Nixon in the 1960 presidential election, and which had increased his popularity among voters. Dad believed in analyzing and learning from the past. To many Southern states, including South Carolina, textiles—the production of fabrics—made up the lifeline which drove the economy and kept good-hearted Southern Americans employed. By committing to support textiles before his opponents did, Nixon gained key votes from the South.

As soon as Nixon moved into the White House, the battle over textiles began. But he delivered what he had promised. After much deliberation, which included diplomatic visits to Japan, Nixon set forth his bold economic policy on August 15, 1971. He established wage and price controls, and placed a surcharge on imports. The successful conclusion of the textile agreements in October of 1971 was hailed by Paul Clancey of the *Philadelphia Inquirer* as "one of the greatest single political strokes for Richard Nixon in the South since he landed the White House."[12]

My father went with the president's envoy on some of those trips to the Far East. If something concerned the South, Harry Dent was right in the middle of it.

Balancing the Courts

One of the issues that attracted my dad to Nixon during the 1968 campaign was Nixon's pledge to put conservatives on the US Supreme Court. The two men shared a grave concern about the leftward tilt of the Court. Nixon and my father both wanted judges who would respect the Constitution and not rewrite it. The president felt that the most important and enduring effect he could have on this country would be through balancing the Supreme Court.[13]

Nixon's first appointment to the high court was Chief Judge Warren Burger of the US Court of Appeals. When another vacancy came open, my father submitted the name of Judge Clement Haynsworth of the Fourth Circuit of Appeals. When Judge Haynsworth's nomination was eventually rejected (although supported by Senator Fritz Hollings, a longtime Democrat from South Carolina), Nixon charged my dad to find another conservative judge from the South. My father searched until he found Judge Harrold Carswell of Florida—but after another bitter battle, Carswell too was denied the nomination. Nixon finally realized the liberal Senate wouldn't confirm a Southerner.

Nixon made a statement to the Senate on the rejection of two Southern men in a row: "Judges Haynsworth and Carswell have endured with admirable dignity vicious assaults on their intelligence, their honesty, and their character . . . and they had the misfortune of being born in the South."[14] He had no recourse but to go outside the South, and eventually Judge Harry Blackmun of Minnesota was confirmed.

Nixon finally got the chance to confirm a Southerner when Justice Hugo Black from Alabama died during Nixon's first term. Lewis Powell of Virginia was given the honor of filling the vacated position. It was one Southerner for another. Assistant Attorney General William Rehnquist, a conservative ideologue, was also appointed and confirmed at the same time. Newspapers were reeling with headlines like, "Two Conservatives Appointed to the Supreme Court." The impact of a president being able to name four men to the Supreme Court, all of whom were "conservative" on crime issues, helped tilt the court back into balance, just as my father and Nixon had hoped.

President Nixon summed up well his courtship with the South: "As for this Southern Strategy stuff—all we're doing is treating the South with the same respect as the North."[15]

The War in Vietnam

Among the main attractions to Richard Nixon for Southerners were his anti-Communist record and his sense of patriotism to our country, along with his commitment to freedom. Southerners, both black and white, were fiercely loyal patriots and were strongly anti-Communist. That is why there were so few antiwar demonstrations in the South during the Vietnam War. The qualities in Nixon that repelled many in the Northeast were the very things that attracted many in the South, including his prosecution of Alger Hiss (a US government worker alleged to be a Communist spy) in the 1940s and '50s, his support for a strong national defense and his gift for foreign policy.

Although he was anti-Communist, in the summer of 1969 President Nixon began US troop withdrawals from Vietnam. In doing this, he was not giving in to the Communists in Southeast Asia. Instead, he was trying to appease the antiwar protesters who were getting out of hand at home. But Nixon wanted "peace with honor," so even in the midst of troop withdrawals, he took strong action in Southeast Asia when he had to. When he did, the national polls showed a drop in support—but never in Dixie.

On April 30, 1970, Nixon announced on national television his order to send American and South Vietnamese troops into Cambodia to destroy enemy supplies and equipment in a surprise attack. In the days before his announcement, he brought my father into his office as he was contemplating his decision. He told my father that what he was planning to do would stir up the protestors, and he wondered how the Southern people would react.

My father's response was emphatic: "Mr. President, you can count on the South. We've stood by you on Vietnam, and we'll continue to do so with whatever action you deem necessary to end the war with honor." That was the exact disposition of the Southern states. No one knew the South better than my father—he was one of their own, born and bred.

The Cambodian decision was never fully accepted in the States, but in the end it helped to shorten the war as enemy supplies took a heavy hit with the surprise attacks. It was rare, whenever I visited the White House during this time, not to encounter antiwar protesters. People continued protesting until the official withdrawal of all troops, which came later.

President Nixon decided to bomb North Vietnam in December of 1972 when they backed away from their agreement to allow America to leave with honor. In early 1973 American prisoners of war came home singing the president's praises. Nixon had finally ended the war in Vietnam without surrender, and with the return of our American boys.

President Nixon's ratings in the South soared even higher than when he had won the entire South in the 1972 election. When Nixon visited Columbia to thank the people for their unwavering support of his Vietnam policies, the South Carolina General Assembly gave him a hero's welcome. Nixon was also well aware that more Southerners volunteered for military service than did people from any other part of the country, and he knew they had paid a price for their support. Although Nixon was continually criticized by the left wing about a war he had not started, in my father's eyes, and throughout much of the South, he ended the war with honor.

No one was more elated to see the war ended than my family. Both my boyfriend Alton and my oldest brother Harry Jr., when they turned nineteen, had drawn low numbers in the draft. When Alton had shown up to be examined and drawn his low number, the sergeant had told him, "Son, we'll be seeing you soon." But Nixon's withdrawals and his reliance upon the volunteer army had reduced the number of young men being drafted. The war was over before they had to go.

Nixon courted the South during his time in office, and as far as my father was concerned, he won her over. He delivered what he had promised—and as a result, the South was no longer treated like a stepchild. Desegregation was finally achieved successfully and without force, textiles were protected, the Supreme Court was balanced, and the Vietnam War was finished. The South, and the nation, would let their feelings be known in the 1972 presidential election.

4

GOOD THINGS FROM BAD THINGS

My parents had raised me well. Moral training was important to them, and an integral part of being brought up in the Dent household. I knew the difference between right and wrong from the get-go. I kept my promise to be a good girl—my mom always made us promise to be good—and I stayed away from alcohol and drugs. I never dated until I was fifteen years old. I can remember the first time I had to ask a guy to a sorority dance. I was so shy that a girlfriend called the number for me, and then I hung up the phone before he answered. Usually, when I wanted to go to a dance, a friend would agree to go with me at the last minute. I wasn't interested in the popular guys necessarily. I wanted someone with character.

My dad was a man of character. He was a living example of integrity every day of my life. There was no one I loved or honored more than my father. My father loved to dance, and he taught me. Cutting the rug with my dad was one of my joys as a teenager. He would whirl me around the floor, smiling from ear to ear. He loved to tease me, saying that one day I would marry my prince, and his name would be Elmer Snodgrass. *Elmer Snodgrass?*

At Dreher High School I was what some would call "an unimportant little sophomore" with no status. But I attended all the high-school events, and there was one guy in particular who

I noticed. He was on the football and basketball teams. When I noticed him following me to my classes, I would sheepishly hide from him in the bathroom. On December 31, 1970, he asked me to dance with him at a New Year's Eve party. His name wasn't Elmer. It was Alton Brant, and he was a Big Man on Campus. He was captain of the football team, a starter on the basketball team, an officer of the senior class and a heck of a dancer! After that party he began calling me. But boy, did he have a lot of coaxing to do to get me to go out with him. I finally agreed, and it was the first of many dates.

Although it seemed a tragedy at first, my move to Dreher High School turned out to be something God used for good. I got to know many of the black athletes there while I was dating Alton. Dreher had gradually desegregated and was making excellent progress in that regard. Sports were the main thing that brought blacks and whites together. Teamwork has a way of doing that. My election as cheerleader by the student body at the end of my sophomore year was probably due to students of both races saying, "Vote for her. She's Alton's girl." I can assure you it wasn't because I was the most coordinated contestant!

Yes, in time I made the adjustment to Dreher, my former rival high school. My life didn't come to a stop when I moved there, but rather it continued to blossom. Later I would see that my sister and I were part of an important social change influencing the course of progress toward desegregation. A change that needed to happen.

By age sixteen I had the world by the tail, or so my father would have said. I was president of my high-school sorority, first runner-up Miss Sophomore, May Court attendant and girlfriend of a senior who was captain of the football team, and I had plenty of friends. My modeling career was flourishing with television commercials and weekly photo shoots. If that weren't enough, my father worked for the president of the United States.

Another Transition

My whole world came crashing in again when my father announced, several weeks after I was elected varsity cheerleader, that we would all be moving back to Washington as soon as school was out for the summer. My father had been working in the White House for two years now and had commuted to Washington from South Carolina, coming home on the weekends. He had hoped we wouldn't have to move, but his job was keeping him so busy that he could no longer come home to see us. For the sake of our family, we needed to live in the same city.

In Columbia everything had gone my way. In Washington DC I was about to find that nothing would go my way.

I left behind all my friends, my boyfriend, my honors and accomplishments, and in the fall of 1971 I started my junior year at Langley, my third high school. The school had three thousand students and was featured in *Newsweek* as the "High School Drug Capital of the US." You can imagine how my parents felt when they read that just two weeks after we had moved. The immorality in this high school far exceeded anything I had ever seen. The affluent community called McLean, which was known as the DC home of the Kennedy's, was filled with sexual freedom, abortions, drugs, drinking, materialism, suicides and alienation between children and their parents. I had never seen anything like this before. Peer pressure had been bad in some areas in Columbia, but not to this extreme.

As a result, I had nothing in common with anyone, nor did I have any real friends, not even in the church we attended. So I spent my time working on the only thing that made me feel good about myself—modeling. I also spent some time with Senator and Nancy Thurmond. They continued to be like family to us. They had just given birth to their first daughter, Nancy Moore Thurmond. Sometimes on the weekend I would babysit for them. Nancy was one of the cutest babies I had ever held in my arms.

It was a very lonely year for everyone in my family. We had

all given up so much to move to Washington, and we had done it to be with our father. Yet he was rarely home. If I wanted to be with him, I had to go to work with him or travel with him just like I had when I was younger.

Anytime Air Force One was flying to Columbia, I made every effort to be on the plane. The Nixons were always cordial and welcomed me as I boarded the plane. I remember tagging along when President Nixon went to the funeral of former South Carolina Governor James Byrnes. Instead of thinking how wonderful it would be to fly with President and Mrs. Nixon, I was thinking how great it would be to visit my friends and my boyfriend back in Columbia. The most memorable event in that trip was seeing the newspaper reporters and the masses of people waiting for the president's plane as we arrived at Columbia Metropolitan Airport. My friends were there to pick me up as well—just in smaller numbers.

My father taught me early in life that all people are basically the same. Whether someone was the president of the United States or an average person on the street, they all had the same worries and problems to deal with in life. Each morning they put their pants on the same way—one leg at a time. Although I respected the office of the presidency, I never saw the Nixons as anything but two people who were serving the American people. As far as my father was concerned, all politicians were to be servants of the people first. They were never to use their power in any misguided way. That's a lesson I haven't forgotten.

An Intended Demotion

This story turns on moments large and small. During that year while attending Langley High School, I had a part-time, after-school job modeling in the DC area. When assignments took me downtown, I would drop into Dad's office in the East Wing to have lunch or dinner with him in the White House dining room. On one of those trips, I tore past the East entrance, as always, and swung right, as always—right into a wrong office.

My dad's Palmetto-tree curtains, South Carolina flag and aquarium were all missing in action. Pivoting back toward the door, my eyes began to scan the words "Office for First Lady Pat Nixon" just as I heard the out-of-context voice of Mrs. Nixon's secretary saying, "Your father is in the Executive Office Building now."

Whatever. I was painfully, typically sixteen—no overstating that. My interests fell across the four broad categories of school, boyfriend, church and modeling. Happening onto this relocation meant learning a new route. Big deal. But this detour—we learned later that my dad's change of office signaled a demotion—would prove bigger than any of us imagined. One day soon my family would revere it, mark the date, celebrate it as Dad's road around a prison sentence.

A Change Begins

As bad as things were in Washington, I did find something good there. I got involved in a Young Life group. Young Life was the only group I found that generated a positive form of peer pressure. Through Young Life and through the teaching of Tom Raley, the Young Life director in McLean, Virginia, I began to understand more clearly the true message of the Christian life. It was the first time I understood that Jesus wanted to be not only my Savior, but also the Lord of my life—that Christ was more than just fire insurance. I learned that I could have a personal relationship with Him and that He had a plan for my life (and boy, did He).

On New Year's Eve, 1971, I realized for the first time that my Christian faith had been merely circumstantial. It depended on how things went and how people treated me. That New Year's Eve I was in the hospital, recovering from a tonsillectomy. While lying in bed all alone that night, I looked out at the beautiful full moon, and the majesty of the sky touched me deeply. Simply lying there, quietly reflecting, I surrendered my life to Jesus. My heart was changed, and I realized that the God who created such a beautiful and orderly universe had sent His only Son to die for my sins.

I might not have looked like a very sinful person, but the book of James says that "whoever keeps the whole law and yet stumbles at just one point is guilty of breaking all of it" (2:10). My biggest sin had been trying to run my own life in my own strength—being my own God. I had done just fine, until I couldn't control all the circumstances of my life.

The Gospel of John says, "For God so loved the world that he gave his one and only Son, that whoever believes in him shall not perish but have eternal life" (3:16). What we often miss in this well-recited verse is that the word "believe" means much more than mere acknowledgment. We must do more than just acknowledge, for even the devil acknowledges that Jesus is God—so much so that he trembles. In believing, we must commit our hearts, souls and minds to the Lord. That night in the hospital room, I realized my plan of getting to heaven by my good works wasn't going to work. That night I began trusting Jesus with my life, depending on His sacrifice for my salvation and following His purpose for my life.

After that change, God began working in my life, teaching me truths about myself through Bible studies at Young Life. I began a daily discipline of prayer and Bible study. I certainly had a lot to learn. From those studies I grew spiritually—and one thing I suddenly realized was that my boyfriend from Columbia, Alton Brant, whom I so dearly loved and was still seeing, was a decent person, but he wasn't a Christian.

It was deeply important to me that my boyfriend and I share the same faith. So although it was very difficult for me to do, I ended the relationship. I explained to Alton the spiritual decision I had made, and I challenged him to ask God to reveal Himself to him. This was one of the hardest things I had ever had to do up to that point in my life. Alton was the only stability I had. Although he was five hundred miles away, he had given me a level of confidence I had never experienced before. All I knew to do was pray for him.

Now I really had to depend upon the Lord, and He became the only stable force in my life.

A Material Girl and the Mafia

From the time I was twelve years old, my heart's desire, like that of many young girls, was to become a model. I had dreamed of going to New York City to work and, one day, open my own modeling studio. That was a lofty goal for an introvert. But having attended three elementary schools and three (so far) high schools and moving six times, I had been forced out of my shell. So during my junior year in Washington I continued my modeling career by attending John Robert Powers Modeling School for further training. I registered myself with a major modeling agency in DC, which landed me jobs in the afternoons and on weekends.

I was elated when I was offered a contract to be on the cover of a magazine based in DC. I had gone in for the test shots and was a given a long contract to sign before the cover issued could be released. Since I was only sixteen, I had been given strict orders by my father to bring any written contract straight to him, the ever-thinking attorney. He looked over this one with a raised eyebrow. I could tell there was something he didn't like.

"We'll discuss it later," he said, and he put it in his briefcase. The following day he decided it was time for a father-daughter night on the town. He cleared his Saturday evening and took me to dinner at the famous DC steakhouse, Black's—just the two of us. I was wondering what I had done to deserve this. We had a great time at Black's, where you could order your steak exactly the way you wanted it. Mary Poppins once said that a spoonful of sugar helps the medicine go down; I think my dad felt that a big chunk of tasty steak might do the same thing for me.

After dinner he took me to a movie. The movie wasn't exactly what I would have planned for a father-daughter night on the town: he took me to see *The Godfather*. I was horrified at all the violence. "Can you believe some people think things like that really happen?" I said in innocent amazement. But my father had chosen that movie for a reason. He needed to shock me out of my naiveté in order to explain why he couldn't allow me to sign that contract—and my mind was not even in the ballpark. He took me to an ice cream shop (his favorite splurge) on the way home and pulled out the contract. I'll never forget what he said that night.

"*The Godfather* is fiction, but the Mafia is real. There are people out there who want to be able to bribe me because of my position in the White House, and they can try to do it through my children—my most prized possessions. They can try to get to me by getting to you." Then he told me he had asked a friend at the FBI to check out the magazine for any suspicious connections. It turned out that there was a possibility they were connected to the Mafia. He then showed me the line in the contract where it said they had my permission to use any part of my picture with any other picture. That clause wasn't in my other contracts.

Quite honestly, I still did not understand what he was saying. All I knew was that he wouldn't allow me to sign the contract the way it was written. My dad, fearing there could be a plan behind it, blocked me from my first magazine cover.

Being the compliant child I was, I obeyed, but I didn't understand. I thought my father was losing his marbles and seeing things that weren't there. I can see now that he had my best interest at heart. I've happened to see *The Godfather* a couple times in the last few years. It is certainly not my favorite movie, but whenever I see it, I will always remember that eye-opening night with my father.

New York or Bust!

A few months later, as the summer of 1972 was getting underway, I was granted interviews with Eileen Ford of the Ford Modeling Agency as well as with Wilhelmina Cooper of the Wilhelmina Modeling Agency, both in New York City. I was more impressed with Eileen Ford, and I was offered an opportunity to model with her agency. This was what I had always dreamed of—it was a chance of a lifetime.

Now I had a decision to make. Because I had enough credits from an earlier summer school session, I could graduate from high school early and join the agency in the fall, or I could graduate from high school on schedule and join them after that. Either way, I would live with Eileen Ford and her husband in their penthouse (something they offered to all their new models) until I found friends to room with. That arrangement definitely made my parents feel better about my living in the Big Apple at sixteen.

While I worked through my decision in DC, the Ford Agency sent me to a top-notch photographer for some test shots. As I glanced around at his display of modeling photographs, I suddenly felt strange. I remember being shocked by the revealing poses. My modeling days in Columbia had been much more innocent—Ruth Anne Collins and her agency had made sure of it. I was beginning to see that modeling in New York City wasn't the same as what I had been trained to do. I determined, though, that I could be different.

But when I had met some of Ford's and Wilhelmina's models during my interview trip, one of them had told me that modeling in New York was all about with whom you slept. I didn't want to believe her, but it made me wonder if I really wanted to pursue this as a career.

After much prayer and consideration, I decided to wait a year before moving to New York City. I wanted to have my senior year in high school—and, quite frankly, some of what I had seen in New York unnerved me. Something in my spirit told me I wasn't ready for it yet.

Following my interviews in New York City, I began preparation for a trip to England for a summer foreign exchange program. The school I attended in the UK was the Richard Taunton School for Boys. Yes, boys. I was the only girl there. I think they thought the name on my application was Jimmy. Living in England gave me not only the opportunity to be on my own, and thus truly depend upon the Lord, but also to experience another culture. (While in Europe I was also able to stay for a week at the American Embassy in Paris and explore France. Sometimes it helps to have a dad who works for the president of the United States.) While overseas, even though I had set aside my relationship with Alton, I really missed him, and I continued to pray that God would open the eyes of his heart.

My dad and I were both realizing our dreams. My father was working in the White House defending the freedoms of the nation, and I was on my way to becoming a model in New York City. Despite my concerns about what might go with the job, I wasn't ready to give up that dream quite yet. After all, both of us were exceeding our expectations. Behind the scenes, God was lovingly taking the challenging adjustments in my life and using them for my good. I was on top of the world, not knowing what lay ahead.

5

TURNING TOWARD HOME AND FAMILY

After my trip to England, my family moved, once again, back to Columbia. Because my father was a workaholic, his demanding job in the White House had pushed my mother to the edge of an emotional breakdown.

My mother had come from a broken home. Her father left when she was six years old, leaving her, her mother and her fifteen-year-old sister destitute. His leaving not only crushed them financially, but it emotionally held my mother in bondage, even into her adult years.

A complete hysterectomy in her early thirties caused my mom to have physiological changes at a time before hormone replacement therapy was fine-tuned. She was thrown into the "change of life" stage while she was still young—she was a thirty-six-year-old living in a fifty-year-old's body. Eventually, my mother lost her last hope when the number one man in her life—my father—was never home to rescue her. So the busiest time for my father became one of the darkest for my mother.

A workaholic husband wasn't what she needed. And she didn't know, at that time, that there was a spiritual refuge she could turn to—she wouldn't know true freedom for quite some time yet. My mom began losing her grip. So in an effort to save his marriage and his wife, my father left the White House at the height of his career and, notably, just before the Watergate scandal broke out. I will never forget the night he came into my room to tell me his plan and ask my opinion.

"Your mother is having a difficult time. Things started downhill after her hysterectomy," he began.

"I've noticed she isn't herself," I replied. "But don't you think in time she'll get back on top?"

"I thought so at first," he admitted concernedly, "but now I'm beginning to wonder. It's been six months since her surgery, and her continued depression really concerns me. I'm thinking of moving her back to Columbia where she has friends and family close by. Maybe then she'll begin to make progress."

"You mean you would give up all you've accomplished here and go back home? You would leave your job?"

"My job is partly to blame for her condition, Ginny. I'm never home, and now she needs me more than ever. I can't serve the president and take care of her needs. She comes first. If I can get her back in familiar territory and into a more normal life, then maybe her condition will get better. I'll just have to do as much as I can from South Carolina and commute when I have to. But I need to know how you feel about moving to another high school again."

I was stunned. He would give up all he had accomplished for the sake of my mother. We both saw her sinking and being pulled down with the current. I really hated the thought of moving again, but when I saw the seriousness of my mother's depression, I too felt we needed to go back to Columbia.

In looking back, I realize that not many men would give up their political careers for their spouse. Although my father was guilty of workaholism in the first degree, he was never a politician who allowed his ego to get in the way of his family. When he sensed my mother sliding into the dark abyss of depression, he gave it all up to rescue her. That was the kind of man he was.

Making Adjustments—Again

When we moved back to Columbia in the fall of 1972, my

parents decided to rent an apartment for us to live in while they had a new home built. We lived in a different school district than before, so for my senior year I went to Spring Valley High—my fourth high school. By this time I was half loony, and definitely more outgoing. I continued my modeling career and began to teach modeling and self-improvement courses with my Columbia friend and mentor, Ruth Anne Collins. Ruth Anne was a successful beauty queen and model who ran her own modeling agency and studio.

Young Life had started a program in the Columbia high schools just the year before, so I was able to continue with their Bible studies. The leader of Young Life at my high school was a very dedicated Columbia International University student named Aaron Fleming. Aaron, along with Bob Metcalf, another Young Life leader, held weekly studies for us. God began to teach me through those studies that I wasn't to model physical beauty. As I grew as a Christian, I began to realize that the inner qualities were far more important and that I was to model Christ in everything I did. God began to teach me about true beauty—from the inside out.

In the first months of my senior year, my mother's depression got worse instead of better. My little brother Jack and I were already enrolled in school in South Carolina when we realized that my mother would require more intensive therapy. My father continued his commitment to Nixon, but he made himself available to be close to my mother during her therapy and medical treatment. When push came to shove, nothing was more important to him than his wife and his family.

The job he held was the kind that demanded all, making it hard for anyone to do the work well and still be the right kind of husband and father. In retrospect, I can see that he was beginning to turn away from all he'd worked for when he was at the top of his career. He gave up a lot to be at my mother's side. I see now that the Washington political lifestyle has made family life difficult for very many.

So at seventeen years old I began to help care for my ten-year-old brother and took on more responsibilities at home. At that time in America, people didn't talk about the D word—depression—and so our family kept that secret to ourselves. I didn't understand what was happening to my mother, and I also didn't understand the complications that growing up in a dysfunctional home like hers could bring. All we knew was that we wanted her to get better, and her recovery became the focus of everything we did. So I continued my "unspoken requests" for prayer at Young Life. The taboo went deep.

Since I couldn't talk to anyone, the only way I knew to help my parents was to watch my brother and pray for my mother's recovery. Many times I also read her passages from the Bible. (She later told me what an encouragement those Scripture readings were to her.)

During my senior year my parents sometimes had to be away overnight. My brother missed our mom terribly when she was gone, and I can remember on one occasion taking him to the emergency room with stomach pains, which turned out to be "I miss my mommy" pains. After that, I kept him closer to me. I took him along to Young Life meetings—and I even took him on dates with me. Several times I asked my dates, "Do you mind if my little brother comes along?"

The only guy who didn't mind was my former boyfriend Alton. He and I still hung out occasionally. He was the only one I could confide in about what was really going on with my family. Jack preferred Alton to the other boys. My little brother was very opinionated—but Alton got a perfect ten rating from him.

Changing Influences

Although my father had moved us back to Columbia to help my mother, he was still away from home a lot, commuting to finish out his four-year term as an advisor to President Nixon. My father was also part of CREEP, a regrettable acronym for the Committee to Reelect the President, working hard to win another term for President Nixon. As had been the case in the 1968 elections, the man who could stand in the way of Nixon's reelection was George Wallace—if he decided to run again.

In 1966 Wallace had helped his wife get elected as governor of Alabama to get around the state law prohibiting a governor from succeeding himself. She held the title, but he controlled the reins. My father could always read the writing on the wall, and he knew the key to Wallace's possible run for the 1972 presidency lay in whether or not he could regain his governorship in 1970. But Wallace lost his grip on it when his precious wife, Lurleen, died of cancer on May 7, 1968, after just two years in office.

Alabama Lieutenant Governor Albert Brewer, George Wallace's protégé, became acting governor. Now if Brewer defeated Wallace in the 1970 election for governor of Alabama, Wallace wouldn't make a run for the presidency again. After losing in the 1968 presidential run, losing the governor's race would weaken him too much politically.

In the election results Brewer led Wallace by 2 percent in the primary, but he hadn't gotten a majority of votes, as required by law, because it was a crowded field. So there was a runoff election. In the end, George Wallace took back his prized possession—the governorship of Alabama, and his hopeful stepping stone to the White House. My father was highly tuned to everything, including polls and election results, and kept the president up to speed on every detail. Dad received the election results after 11:00 p.m. on the runoff night. He decided not to awaken the president, but Nixon was anxious and called my dad on a White House hotline connected directly into our home to get the much-awaited results. Nixon and my dad then knew that Wallace would be a problem again in 1972.

George Wallace had long talks with Nixon and my dad about his plans for the future. He finally told a news reporter in June of 1971 that "if President Nixon would end the war in Vietnam, settle the economy, take care of unemployment, and straighten out this school mess," then he wouldn't run.[1] That was a tall order for Nixon to fulfill in just four years. Needless to say, it sounded like Wallace would run again. And he did, but this time in the Democratic primary.

Wallace's momentum was slowed when on May 15, 1972, he was shot while speaking in Laurel, Maryland. He survived the assassination attempt but was confined to a wheelchair. He became a wounded national hero overnight, but the extra support wasn't enough. His candidacy was rejected at the Democratic National Convention in Miami. Not willing to give up, he once again looked into a possible run with the American Independent Party. When the third-party ticket also rejected him as their candidate, Nixon and my father's worst nightmare was finally over. The one man who could stop Nixon from being reelected had finally been restrained.

Thank goodness. Now my dad would be able to spend some time with his family, at least for a while.

6

WATERGATE—
THE
BEGINNING

On Sunday, June 13, 1971, a confidential Defense Department report on the Vietnam War was bursting into national newspapers. The top-secret report, written in part by Daniel Ellsburg and eventually known as the "Pentagon Papers," detailed the US political-military involvement in Vietnam between 1945 and 1967. Ellsburg, believing that the study "demonstrated unconstitutional behavior by a succession of presidents," leaked the papers to the press in an effort to bring the Vietnam War to a close.

Former White House Special Counsel Chuck Colson has famously said that the scandal that took a presidency started in the White House Roosevelt Room. The "Cabinet Room," as it is called, is a door away from the Oval Office. The day after Ellsburg's report hit newsstands, President Nixon called a special meeting of his senior staff in this room. My father wasn't present at that meeting because he was in South Carolina—and he wasn't invited.

There are a couple of key points to know about the infamous Pentagon Papers. It was completed in 1968, *before* Richard Nixon became the nation's thirty-seventh president. Furthermore, the report was highly critical of Presidents Johnson and Kennedy, but not of Nixon. It was the leak itself and not the report that panicked Nixon, who was by this time compulsively eager to end the war. His anxiety must have been contagious, for the men in the cabinet meeting that day formed a special covert task force that would come to be known as the Plumbers. The Plumbers' job was to stop further leaking of classified information; they would answer to several high-ranking aides who were members of CREEP.

The Plumbers masterminded the two 1972 Watergate burglaries—on May 28 and again on June 17. Their goal was to bug the offices of the Democratic National Committee, located in the Watergate Hotel. It all happened about the same time that I was sunbathing at the posh hotel complex. Although the five burglars were arrested immediately, it wasn't until October of 1972 that the FBI began closing in on the Plumbers. Investigators had discovered that the break-ins were political espionage on behalf of CREEP, to which my dad belonged.

One month later, in almost Shakespearean irony, President Nixon carried more than 60 percent of the popular vote and forty-nine of fifty states in the Electoral College. It was one of the largest presidential landslides in American history. But it was too late. The unraveling was underway.

Instead of rising to a national mandate, Richard Nixon began a personal and public slide into evasions, lies, missing tapes, impeachment threats and resignation. Twenty-five of his twenty-seven aides and cabinet members would be convicted of crimes and would spend time in prison. Chuck Colson, and later my father, believed that the presidency could have survived the break-in but that the real scandal—what brought down a US president and his aides—was their massive effort to cover it up.

My Father's Last Days with Nixon

After thanking his cabinet and staff members after his landslide reelection, Richard Nixon directed Chief of Staff Bob Haldeman to fire everyone. The president wanted to reorganize his staff for this second term. Then he retreated to Camp David for several weeks to put together his new team. Those who were asked to stay on would be flown to Camp David on Marine

One to get their new assignment. My father had already given his resignation a few months earlier, when we had moved back to South Carolina, so he was surprised when he got the call to go to Camp David.

Although working for Nixon had been the greatest and most exciting experience of his life, he knew that his commitment to stay in Columbia must stand. At Camp David the president begged him to stay on, but there was no reversing his decision. Family commitments trumped the president. Another concern of my dad's was his uneasy feeling about how John Ehrlichman, chief domestic advisor, and Bob Haldeman, chief of staff, were running the White House. The duo was known jointly as "The Berlin Wall" by White House staff members, partly due to their inclination to isolate the president from other aides who wanted to speak with him. As much as my dad wanted to stay with Nixon, he needed to leave.

Nixon didn't give up on my dad, though, and on December 8, 1972, they met again at Camp David's Aspen Lodge for what was supposed to be a short meeting. Nixon offered him the position of assistant attorney general. He assumed that with my dad's background as an attorney, he would be honored. My father *was* honored, but for a second time he declined an offer from the president because of his commitment to his family. Instead, he agreed to work as general counsel for the Republican Party's National Committee—a part-time position he could carry out from Columbia.

When the topic turned to the looming scandal of Watergate, the "short" meeting turned into an extended discussion. My father was candid with his advice. He told Nixon that he believed things could become uncorked. He emphasized to the president his place in history, including all he had accomplished in foreign policy, and warned him that Watergate could ruin it all. He encouraged Nixon to remove immediately anyone who was under any suspicion and to ask the nation's forgiveness for what had happened in his administration. My father believed that with

Nixon's overwhelming popularity, the American people would have forgiven him.[1]

Nixon, however, didn't take my father's advice.

A Daughter's Support

Shortly after Sam Donaldson aired his public accusation against my father and Chuck Colson in March of 1973, saying they had masterminded the Watergate break-in, Dad and I drove to the Waffle House, a regular haunt of ours. I know Dad never intended to cry in front of me that night or to say all he said. But with my mom still recovering from her physical illness and depression, he had no one else to confide in. We had the restaurant to ourselves. It's funny how particular details about key events stay with you. I remember the metal chair scraping loudly against the floor because it was missing a rubber tip. I remember fingering the cold ridges in the table rim as Dad told me that he couldn't expect a fair trial in Washington DC.

"The TV and what Sam Donaldson said . . . I know it's confusing. But what they're saying about me is not true, Honey. Donaldson doesn't know what he's talking about. I can't be sure who he's talking to, but he's got the story wrong. I had nothing to do with that break-in."

I stared at the man speaking. Who was this stranger, so shaken and pale? I told him I believed none of it, but he seemed hardly to notice.

"Things are rough," he said, clasping his hands on the table's edge. "Working in this White House is an engraved invitation to problems with Cox." He was referring to Archibald Cox, the Watergate special prosecutor.

"This is America, Dad," I replied earnestly. "You're innocent until proven guilty."

"Not this round, sweetie," he smiled weakly. "The finger points to every person on Richard Nixon's staff, and that includes your ol' dad."

My stomach started to tighten. "Everyone knows you're

honest!" I said loudly. And when I did, the hollow laugh that came from my father was something I'd never heard before.

"A lot of smart people are in top gear, and the stakes are high," he said. He let out a long breath, but it seemed to give him no relief. "They're making history, and it's hard to fight them. I've got to hire a defense attorney. My defense could cost us everything we own. This is going to be hard on all of you."

He looked at me with tears streaming down his face. "I never dreamed that Washington would end like this. If the worst happens and I'm convicted, I won't be allowed to practice law, Ginny. My license will be revoked."

Then our eyes met and we both shivered at the same thought: *What would this do to my mom's recovery?*

"I never meant for my political life to hurt any of you, especially your mother."

I had a brother and a sister in college, and I was in my senior year of high school. Over the Waffle House's spattered yellow Formica table, my father, the Nixon White House staffer, was finishing a sentence with the words ". . . no tuition payments from prison."

Oh my . . . oh my. I pushed at the rising chaos in me. "You are a lawyer—defend yourself, Dad," I said. "God knows and sees everything. He'll prove a person right if he's innocent." I leaned forward and quoted Romans 8:31: "If God is for us, who can be against us?"

"But Ginny, you're too young and naive to understand there will be no fair trial for me in Washington. Not with all that has happened."

"I'm naive enough to know that there are times when all we can do is trust in God."

"Ginny, this is a time when I need for you to be strong . . . no matter what happens."

Then Dad was so quiet that I could hear the sounds in the kitchen. I wasn't prepared to watch this man unravel. After a short while he pushed up from the table, and we walked to the parking lot. My stomach was in knots all the way up to my throat.

In my head I prayed. The next day, at every opportunity, I begged people I knew to pray. At weekly Young Life Bible studies, I submitted more "unspoken" prayer requests, meaning I couldn't give them details of what was keeping me awake nights. When I read the Bible, verses I had skipped over in the past, messages about suffering and trust and valleys, now stood out and shouted to me. This was more than I could face, and, adding to the internal pressure, I couldn't unload to my friends.

Dad asked me to help with my mom and my little brother, Jack, if he ended up being sent to prison. I was already helping look after Jack, of course, while Mom and Dad continued to travel back and forth between South Carolina and DC for my dad's job and my mom's health needs. I told him he didn't have to ask.

What I Could Never Believe

Once, a reporter seemingly materialized out of nowhere in the parking lot of our apartment complex to shout at me: "What will you do if your father goes to prison?" I just fixed my eyes on the pavement and walked on. This became my default response. Whatever the headline, whatever the whisper, whatever the new sucker punch, I lowered my gaze and pushed through.

It was bad enough that I had to go through the harassment, but I didn't want my little brother to suffer too. Of all the siblings, I was the one closest to home, so I made it my job to shield Jack from the media and the nightly news reports. Now I had another reason to bring him on dates with me.

On some of those dates, to be sure, he was a welcome distraction. While I did my best to avoid the worst of Watergate, my friend Alton made it his job to prepare me for the inevitable. One night our relationship nearly ended on the spot. I remember stopping cold on a path near our house, unsure of what I had just heard from him. "What did you just say?" I spit out.

He had told me that my father couldn't have helped running with the pack. "You love your dad, Ginny. Everyone knows you do. We all think the world of him, but he's human and under unthinkable pressure. You're telling me Sam Donaldson lied on national television?"

"My father," I said coolly to my all-but-former friend, "does not lie. Sam Donaldson can announce scoops until he's blue in the face and until every face around him turns the same color. My . . . father . . . has . . . broken . . . no . . . law."

"All right, all right, Ginny. Every man who worked anywhere near Richard Nixon is being indicted and headed for prison. But your dad is the only innocent one in the group. Your father is the single exception."

I started walking again.

"I love that you see the good in people." Alton pulled on my arm and stopped me. He tried to come around to face me. "This time it's blinding you. Keep your head in the sand, and the truth will run you down. If your dad is guilty, you need to be ready. It's you I care about."

"If you care about me, then never, never, never bring this up again." The temperature between us had dropped forty degrees. We turned and walked back to the house.

After he left that night, it took me a while to cool off. I could feel my heart pounding inside my head. What was he trying to do to me? I still hoped my dad would be cleared. There was still a flicker of light burning through all this darkness, and Alton was trying to blow it out. It took me weeks to get over it. He had pushed my buttons, and I was reeling with anger.

Every family in the White House was snapped in pieces by Watergate. But amid the long hours of pain and suffering, not once did I entertain the idea that Harry Dent was guilty. The world could break around us; I found my hope in God. What peace I had came from prayer and reading the Bible. The more flack I got, the more I read my Bible, and the more I stayed on my knees in prayer. Dad was Dad; I knew who he was. I ignored the accusations and questions, kept my eyes on the pavement and walked on.

Disillusionment

Alone at night, I wasn't nearly as certain of anything. During the weeks and months after the scandal broke, when I would lie in the dark, I often wondered what my family had done to fall into this nightmare. Dad had instilled in me the honor of public service from the time I was born, and I was a true believer in it. My dad had worked hard to get where he was. From the small South Carolina town of St. Matthews, he had risen to serve the most powerful man in the world in Washington DC—but right now the reward felt anything but honorable.

Ever since I had been old enough to sing "My Country, 'Tis of Thee," I had been sure that the white domes stood for everything true and good and just. To a little girl it was a fantastic wonderland of white columns and heroic statues. That place was gone now. The Washington landmarks had turned into landmines, and no one was safe. Before my eyes much of my childhood was slipping away. And there was more to come.

7

DIFFERENT LOOKS, DIFFERENT PERSPECTIVES

Despite the upheaval that the accusations against my father had produced for our family, in the end, my senior year at Spring Valley High School in Columbia turned out to be a great year. In late April of 1973, about a month after he had first reported the accusation against my dad, Sam Donaldson of *ABC World News Tonight* finally apologized on the air and admitted that he had gotten his information from a bad source. This brought immense relief.

In another vein, through Young Life and through Aaron Fleming's mentoring, I had grown spiritually and made many friends. Though I was elected to Homecoming Court and named "Miss Senior" in the high-school pageant, these things weren't as important to me as they once had been. The luster of a shiny new trophy had lost its shine.

Then a very important prayer of mine was answered when Alton gave his life to the Lord about a year after we'd broken up. The most important thing I learned that year was to develop a daily devotional and prayer life. That discipline would see me through a difficult senior year as well as the difficult times ahead.

Also at the end of my senior year, my dear mother was able to return to a more normal life. She was well on her way to recovery, and she was even able to reach out and help other people who were experiencing what she had been through. She took her place on the State Mental Health Advisory Board and volunteered at Contact Help, a volunteer-coordinated hotline that assisted callers who were suicidal or depressed. She later served as its chairman. Eventually, in 1986, she was named one of the ten outstanding "Women of Achievement in Columbia" for her community service work on mental health.

During a time when my father had been giving up his dreams, my mother had been finding hers: in her continuing search for reality in her faith, she had a growing desire to be a godly woman. My parents had always been deeply devoted to each other, but now my mother was newly determined to be supportive. My father had stood by my mother during her difficult times, and now my mother would do the same for him.

Family came first in my life too. I decided not to return to New York City. My family needed me more. My dad and I felt that if I left home, it would pull the rug out from under my mother's feet just when she was beginning to get well. My mom had come a long way, but with her two oldest children already in college, it was important that I be there for her.

We were finally a family again. My dad was no longer commuting to DC. And seeing my mother healthy and with a relaxed smile on her face was the best thing that happened that year. We moved into our newly built home in Spring Valley in the spring of 1973. Things were finally looking up.

Hearing God's Call

That fall I entered Columbia College, the local liberal arts college for women, to study voice and psychology. I learned far more through personal experience, though, than through any textbook. I had a hectic schedule as a full-time student and a fashion merchandising teacher at a local commercial college, and I continued with my modeling career. But college wasn't at all what I expected. I thought it would be a time to date, go to parties and have fun—clean fun, of course. But every time I turned around, the Lord brought someone into my life who was deeply hurting.

My freshman year, two of the girls in my dorm tried to take their own lives, and my closest friend struggled deeply when she lost her mother to cancer. The Lord began to give me a heart for people who were hurting. During my sophomore year, another close friend, who had everything going for her, seemed like she was depressed. It was as if she was smiling on the outside, but agonizing on the inside. One night I dreamed that she had tried to take her own life. The following day I asked her if everything was all right, and she just smiled and said everything was fine. The next morning the dean of Columbia College came to my dorm room to tell me that my friend had taken a bottle of aspirin and walked out onto a busy four-lane highway. The people in the car that almost hit her took her to the hospital.

I realized the Lord was trying to tell me something. The dean told me that my friend, having survived the ordeal, was asking for me. It turned out that her struggle with depression was a long path to healing. Her doctors were able to help her get back on the road to recovery, but what helped her most was our times of reading and studying the Bible together. Today she is a strong Christian and married to a wonderful, sensitive Christian man. If you were to meet her now, you would never believe any of this could have happened to her. As a talented singer and musician, she continues to give her testimony today.

Viewing Life from God's Perspective

My heart was so burdened for this friend and for others like her that, like my father, at the height of my burgeoning career, I decided to give it all up for something more important. Modeling and running my own modeling school and working in the Big Apple—no matter how lucrative—would no longer be my full-time pursuit.

I now put all my efforts toward studying psychology, and I dropped all my modeling contracts practically overnight. I began to see how the modeling industry hurt many people. Those who didn't look like a Barbie doll were often left feeling inadequate. I began to see just how much the modeling industry used sex to sell products. Today I see true beauty as coming from the inside. And I believe this is the way our heavenly Father sees us, for He looks at our hearts and not at our outward appearance.

Now when I meet someone, I focus on their heart and actions, not just their looks. I don't really see them until I get to know them better. Seeing things as God sees them is looking at life through "Heaven's Eyes." This popular song made famous by Sandi Patti eventually became one of my favorite contemporary songs, because "in heaven's eyes there are no losers."

Worldly Desires Fade

The last pageant I modeled in was the "Miss Columbia College" pageant. I was named first runner-up to Jane Jenkins Herlong, who later became Miss South Carolina. Jane was a Christian and used her position as Miss Columbia College to be a witness for Christ. The Lord, however, was leading me in a different direction.

The one thing that had brought me joy and confidence was now slowly dying within me, along with my plans to enter the Miss South Carolina pageant. I simply lost that desire as the Lord gave me a new direction and passion in my life. At that time in my life, I realized I had only been pursuing "worldly success." As a matter of fact, I had become very good at it—my father had trained me very well in that area.

But my Lord wasn't interested in worldly success. Our heavenly Father calls us to be faithful. He is not interested in seeing us fulfill our worldly desires as much as in having us follow His purpose for our lives. That purpose is unique for each person, and only by communicating with God and seeking His will can we find it. I began to see the plan God had for my life, and it wasn't modeling.

My purpose in life would relate to all the experiences I'd had up to that point. My mother's struggle with depression had impacted my life. All the hurting people God set in my path hadn't come along by accident. God had been using my life to help others. Now He spoke to me through my circumstances. My heart was changing, my thoughts were changing, and my direction was changing. God was speaking.

Surrendering one's will to God's plan isn't a one-time thing. Time would teach me that it's a daily thing. It's a process that continues until the Lord calls us home and we truly become His forever. I had a lot to learn about God and His ways, but time would also teach me that the learning never stops. The more I learn about God and His ways, the more my perspective about this world changes. It's not about me. . . . It's about Him.

My Desperate Prayer and Promise

Religion in the South flows in through the drinking water and out through the culture as naturally as sweet tea shows up at lunch and dinner. It's just there. In the Bible Belt—or what was once called the Bible Belt—nary an eyebrow arches when terms like "Bless your heart" or "Where's your church home?" bob and weave through the conversation. Mississippi, Alabama, Georgia, South Carolina . . . here is where Sunday mornings are a bright note after a "dark" Saturday night, where shouts of "Can I get a witness!" come straight down the aisle to the church altar. In my father's South Carolina boyhood in the 1940s and '50s, whether for love of God or because of generations of "That's what we do," Sunday mornings with Jesus were as socially sacred as were Friday nights with the gods of high-school football.

And my dad loved it all. He loved the tradition of Sunday morning church. He loved sitting in the church pews, seeing friends, sharing values and common experiences. Harry S. Dent of St. Matthews, South Carolina, was a big-picture soul who grew up inhaling religion in a big-picture way. As an adult, more than once he summed up the value of church as "a force for moral good"—all the reason a man needed to suit up on Sunday mornings to take in a sermon and sing the beloved hymns that most of the congregation knew by page number and by heart.

It was natural for Dad to help found prayer groups in the US Senate and in the Nixon White House. It was natural for him to live the moral life he picked up at church. Religion was the beam that props, the mortar that seals. But any Southerner understands that *actual* faith can elude many of the churchgoing "faithful." In South Carolina a boy could quite easily grow up earning Sunday school badges for perfect attendance and then see to it that his own kids got their badges—and never get around to "getting God" himself. My father was one of those churchgoers who went more for the social aspect than because of a personal relationship with God.

My mother's formative years in South Carolina had also been shaped by religion, but in wildly different circumstances. A county over from St. Matthews, a little girl named Betty Francis needed God in the worst way. Never mind patent leather accessories or social points. Betty was the daughter of a struggling, single mother and a wandering father who had abandoned them to poverty.

When she was a teenager, a fire burned the family house to the ground. Betty and her mother (her older sister had moved out) survived the blaze, but they didn't have any insurance. The nearby town of St. Matthews took in the straggling remnant of a family and helped them get back on their feet.

Starting over in St. Matthews, Betty sought out God on her own. She walked herself to the church down the street. My mom would tell you now that those Sunday school classes and services helped nourish her hungry soul. She knew she was starving for the attention of a father, and so she sought the heavenly Father, however distant He seemed. She was only using Him to fill an emotional void, but it beat having no father at all.

My own experience with religion was quite different from my parents'. I was Harry and Betty's second daughter, third of four kids, now seventeen years old. My involvement with Young Life, taught me my need for a Savior and how to have a relationship with God. I handed heart and soul to God, and I meant it. I belonged to Him. I got involved in Bible studies, formed Christian friendships and learned to pray. I was deepening my faith.

And yet the more surely I embraced the God of my parents' favorite hymns and the Bible they read, the wider grew the gap between their faith and mine. None of us could say at the time what was happening or how to span the growing divide. I only knew that the God Harry and Betty seemed to have driven past had become my full stop. Religion, for my dad, was all about community, but for me, community was a byproduct. Moral goodness was a byproduct. God alone was the end. The Creator of the universe, who loved me before I had a clue what it meant to know or love Him, was my purpose.

I thought this jibed with everything my parents had taught me to believe. But it was dawning on me, ever slowly, that my parents were attending the feast, but not eating. It was as if my father and I were not dancing to the same beat anymore. I didn't want to "straighten them out." Rather, I wanted to show them what had filled me with joy. I had found a great freedom in God, and I wanted them to experience the peace and purpose on the other side of mere religion. I thought that if I loaded their plates with the truth of the gospel, they would taste what was good—but that repeatedly failed. And we all grew increasingly frustrated.

Godly Wisdom

One day, confused and restless about the breach in my family, I sought out counsel. Alton had begun attending Bible college, and he made an appointment for me with a teacher at the college who specialized in family counseling.

James "Buck" Hatch at Columbia Bible College (later named Columbia International University) was the wisest man I knew. Later, when I ended up attending CIU, I took every class he taught, and I've kept my notes to this day. Buck Hatch was the campus legend, teaching courses on marriage and family, child growth and development, hermeneutics (interpreting the Bible) and the progress of redemption (God's plan threaded through the Old and New Testaments).

Buck Hatch died in 1999. His son, Dr. Nathan Hatch, is president of Wake Forest University. Buck Hatch and his wife knew how to raise kids, and they knew when to let kids raise themselves. More than once he said, "Live it, model it. Let 'em make their own decisions, and they'll value them more." This philosophy was never truer than in matters of faith. I've since seen people in Christian service all over the world attempt to force their beliefs on their children. What usually happens instead is rebellion. Love cannot be forced, whether it is love for another person or love for God. Love is either a personal choice, or it becomes a force that is pushed against.

Buck Hatch had an office in the administration building. There was a chair in the hall outside his office where every semester hundreds of students sat, waiting to seek his advice. I made the trek to the CIU Campus, and Buck Hatch made time for me. I hoped that he would give me the right words to help me reach my parents' hearts.

At the time, his advice confused me. "Hands off," he said. "The gospel, literally 'the good news,' won't force-fit into a life, no matter how you love another person." I stared at the great Buck who was letting me down with cloudy counsel. "Follow God for yourself—your life has to say it." He looked at me, again speaking in that tone of voice he must have patented. "Alone, when you pray," he said, "ask for a peer to come into your parents' lives."

I knew that this was an opportunity for me to obey in faith. Even though I lived in an age when teens resisted authority as nonchalantly as they frayed their bellbottoms and parted their hair down the middle, I genuinely wanted to respect God's authority and my parents. I left Professor Hatch's disappointed, since I had wanted a quick fix, but I also knew that this man was miles ahead of me in knowing how truth operates. So I focused on keeping my hands off my parents' faith.

It was difficult to watch my father as he, with goodwill and amiable disregard, shrunk the God of the universe to an assortment of clichés. "God helps those who help themselves," he would say, unwittingly quoting Ben Franklin. He also frequently talked about the "force for moral good." The first time he tossed that one out—the first time after I was a Christian—I was in the living room, deep into a school assignment. I asked him to explain. I had supposed all my life that the man who brought me up to attend church believed what he heard while he was there. But the "moral good" response affected me practically as if he had told me I was adopted.

A force for moral good?

I might have been young in my faith, but I knew God was not manning a scoreboard of moral perfection, checking our prayer breakfast attendance or our volunteer logbook. The God of the Old and New Testament was in the tender business of drawing flawed people to unconditional love. Moral goodness doesn't come from us—it comes out of knowing Him. *Morality isn't what sent God's only Son to the cross*, I wanted to tell my dad. More wisely, with Buck Hatch's voice ringing in my head, I kept my mouth shut.

Dad couldn't know that his most egregious tests of my hands-off policy came packed in his best intentions. Over Thanksgiving weekend during my freshman year in college, when all four kids were home, Dad announced how much money each child would inherit at his death. I adored my dad above anyone else; I didn't ever want to think of his dying, much less wrap ideas of losing him with what was in it for me. Just as jarring to me was my father's new emphasis on money—counting and amassing it. Dad had grown up without money and gone into public service regardless of it. Why bring it up now, and so coarsely? How long had I known Harry Dent?

Professor Hatch was right about the fact that there is no berating a person into love, and as best I could, I held the course.

I learned to hold my tongue when my dad would drop another of his one-liners at the dinner table. I'd butter a roll or reach for tea. After an evening out for Bible study I would laser-line to my room. My new job was merely (merely!) to walk what I believed without annotating it for my parents.

When I was with my mom and dad, I didn't do battle to convince them of the truth. Away from them, however, I pulled out the heavy artillery. I got on my knees and prayed with fervor. I recruited my Christian friends to help barrage God on behalf of my family and me. That year my father's brother, Bobby Dent, lingered through a difficult death from colon cancer. I was once again reminded of my father's mortality, and the fragile state of his soul shook all of mine. With all my heart I believed that if my dad died not knowing Jesus, *really knowing Him*, we would be eternally apart. And that was unthinkable.

The words I prayed for my father—my actual plea—turned on desperate love, as does the story in this book. Because of my growing faith, I would end up throwing off the plans my father had for me—not because I didn't love him but because my love for him overwhelmed me. You have to know that in order to understand why I went to God so often with this longing that permeated every prayer. I bargained for the person I loved most by offering God the thing I feared most. It was a simple but powerful prayer: *If you will bring my father to know You*, I told God, *then when he has to die, I'll let him go. The pain will be unbearable to me, but I won't be resentful or angry*. I would carry my promise to God close to my heart through the years to come.

8

OF BOY SCOUTS AND HONOR

For the Dents the second half of 1973 was a respite, a relatively idle time with no blindsides from the White House and no daily grenades tumbling out of the *Washington Post*. After Sam Donaldson had aired his public apology, any threats associated with Watergate seemed at an end for Harry Dent.

In that handful of months, for up to hours at a time, the knots in my stomach loosened long enough to remind me what it was like to want to eat. On some nights the hours I slept actually outnumbered the hours I lay awake on a hot pillow, anxious and staring. Years later, my older brother and sister, who had been away at college during that time, were amazed to hear Mom, Dad or me describing the consuming terror. And since we went to great lengths to protect my little brother from the trauma, of all the Dent children, the great anxiety of Watergate had settled mostly on me.

In that short lull I was feeling relieved. I could see Dad sitting in a living room chair, legs crossed, newspaper open in a pre-Watergate posture. I could hear Mom on the phone and know that her anxiety was dropping because of the descending pitch in her voice. We had escaped the clutches of Watergate, hadn't we?

An Unexpected Phone Call

The peace was doomed to end. We had escaped round one

of the Watergate trials, but there was a second round to come. A phone call from the assistant prosecutor came in early spring of 1974, when Dad and I were the only ones home. I answered the phone and then laid the receiver on the counter to go find Dad. He took the call; thirty minutes later he was still talking, still standing, white-faced.

He finally hung up. "Now they're after me," he said.

"Who? *Who?*" I insisted.

"The Watergate special prosecutor—his office just called. They want every person on Nixon's staff. They're after me now, and, like I said before, there's no such thing as a fair trial for a Republican in Washington DC."

John Dean had been among the first group of White House aides investigated in Watergate when, in early 1973, the prosecutors finally began to prove that Nixon's staff was connected to the break-in. When *ABC News* had falsely accused my dad the year before (and around the time Dean was being linked to the scandal), my father had called Dean to get information. He told my dad then, "Don't worry, Harry, you don't show up anywhere in this Watergate mess." But that was of no consolation to my dad now.[1]

It was as if we both sensed a page turning. My family had thought Dad was off the hook, but now reality set in. He was being summoned before the Watergate grand jury.

Trial by Trial

A trial jury's job, in a civil or criminal case, is to determine a defendant's innocence or guilt. But a grand jury, which is typically larger than a trial jury, serves a different purpose. It does not settle innocence or guilt, but instead determines whether a prosecutor's indictments and evidence merit holding a trial in the first place. The prosecution wanted my dad before the grand jury to help build a case to put President Nixon and his White House staff on the witness stand.

My father had planned for this eventuality. He had long before made the decision absolutely to tell the truth. Unless he *knew* of a fact or an incident, there would be no deal, no help, no talking. He would never make assumptions that might impugn a fellow White House staffer. That was Dad's characteristic loyalty; among prosecutors it won him no friends. How, they reasoned (and understandably), could the White House strategist—a mastermind credited with winning the South for Richard Nixon—work alongside Watergate operatives and miss the entire break-in? They were certain that Harry Dent was holding onto the goods.

I have heard it said that the truer someone's defense, the less elaborate the explanation. Whether that's simplistic, I can't say, but I do know that my father's defense shone in its brevity. My dad had resisted earlier suggestions by Nixon's chief of staff, Bob Haldeman, to participate in similar covert operations, Dad told the grand jury. Because of it, Haldeman had exiled my dad from any covert operations. That was Dad's story; that was the truth.

In 1964 President Lyndon Johnson had introduced a taping system to the Oval Office so that he could leave for posterity some colorful cases of his ability to push bills through Congress. When Nixon became president, Johnson encouraged him to keep it up, which he did, believing that all the tapes, full of conversations and phone calls, were protected under executive privilege. When it looked as if the Watergate-related recordings could be a liability, Nixon's attorney, Fred Buzhardt Jr. (my dad's close friend and, like my father, a former assistant to Senator Thurmond), advised him to destroy the conversations before the Supreme Court acted. Nixon might have taken Buzhardt's advice, but Haldeman convinced him the tapes would help his case. I remember my father's comment after he attended Nixon's funeral in San Clemente with Governor Campbell: "The president is dead, but the tapes will live forever."

When the Watergate scandal erupted in March 1973—when Nixon's aides were finally proven to be connected to the break-in ten months earlier—Special Prosecutor Archibald Cox led the indictments. When Cox insisted that Nixon turn over the White House tapes, Nixon ordered Cox's resignation. The attorney general and assistant attorney general both resigned rather than impose the order. Solicitor General Robert Bork finally enforced Nixon's order, leaving a vacancy for Leon Jaworski to step in as Watergate special prosecutor.

Jaworski was the son of immigrants—a young Texas meteor who had entered Baylor University at sixteen and started law school a year later. Before presiding over Watergate, he had prosecuted war criminals in postwar Germany and a Mississippi governor for bucking state integration laws, among other headline courtroom dramas. This was the attorney now laser-locked on gathering evidence to convict a president and his staff—and to head the prosecution in any trials that resulted. Jaworski and his team were cleared to probe into every Nixon aide's work. He didn't just investigate the time surrounding Watergate; he looked into the activity in the early days of President Nixon's first term as well. In my father's case, that was key.

That day in our kitchen, as Dad set the telephone receiver in the cradle, he knew the hunt was on—and he believed his innocence was irrelevant. It had been just a few years since my dad had been demoted and moved out of the East Wing of the White House. At that time he had experienced professional exile and was so humiliated that he couldn't bring himself to tell his family about it. Now that unwanted transfer proved providential.

Make that miraculous.

In Genesis 45 a former slave named Joseph has become prime minister of Egypt. As a powerful potentate, he reencounters his brothers decades after they sold him into slavery, and the brothers are, justifiably, frightened out of their wits. "Not to worry," he says to them in so many words, now with a panoramic picture of his life's blind turns. "What you meant for evil, God meant for good." Joseph's sentiment would soon be my dad's.

Shortly after my dad received that call, Fred Buzhardt uncovered a White House memo from the granite-cut Bob Haldeman to Nixon: "Mr. President," the memo read, "I veto Harry Dent from running the reelection campaign because he is too much of a boy scout." Mystery solved. Haldeman had demanded that my father be looped out of the White House inner circle—and out of Watergate—because he was too clean. The job that almost went to my father went instead to Jeb Magruder, who was later indicted and served time in prison.

Finally, an Indictment

That day in early spring 1974, though, Dad's future was still in the crosshairs, and eventually Jaworski's hardworking prosecutors pulled the trigger. The Watergate investigators had discovered that back in the early part of Nixon's first administration, in 1970, my father's office had misreported a campaign contribution. A campaign contribution technicality wasn't Watergate, and it wasn't covert, but it would do. Dad was indicted.

It's more than a daughter's defense when I say Dad was guilty mostly of ignorance. As the Southern strategist who practiced politics as a high art and as a liaison between the people and the president, Dad's role in the White House fund activity was political intelligence. For example, he helped Haldeman and Nixon decide which candidates were most supportive of the president's policies and should thus receive funds. The error came in what was later called "Operation Townhouse." Jack Gleason, an assistant on my father's fund staff in 1970, failed to follow proper procedures in dispensing of a contributor's stock donation. Dad wasn't aware of the misappropriation of funds, but it happened on his watch. This ultimately caused the forming of a political fundraising committee—which raised a red flag, since technically, this committee had not been properly formed.

My father told US District Judge George Hart that he was unaware of the details of the error and that his role in any violation was inadvertent. He also exclaimed, "I did not consciously or intentionally violate the law."[2] Judah Best, Dad's attorney, argued that the old Corrupt Practices Act, which the prosecution was using against my father, hadn't been enforced in forty years. The law, which has since been repealed and replaced, was outmoded and confusing; furthermore, he explained, Mr. Dent had never touched or handled any of the money.[3] Jack Gleason, who pled guilty, was prepared to testify that my father knew nothing about how the money was set up and that he had not done anything illegal in connection with Operation Townhouse.[4] But according to the law, "the hand of one is the hand of all." All facts pointed to Dad.

On December 11, 1974, before Judge George Hart in the US District Court of the District of Columbia, Dad pled his own case with the help of a law partner, Joe Rogers of Manning, South Carolina, and an attorney friend, Ken Robinson. Both Joe and Ken urged Dad to plead innocent. But on that point Harry S. Dent was going on record doing the right thing. He wanted only to do what was right for his family's sake. Having had no knowledge or intent of violating the reporting law, he said, he pled guilty to a misdemeanor charge.

A fair trial for a Southerner in DC at the time of Watergate was next to impossible. In the courtroom, when he finished telling his side of the story and when prosecutor Charles Ruff offered no rebuttal, Judge Hart banged his gavel. A press-packed crowd waited. In the back of the courtroom, Mom braced for a sentence of up to a year in prison and/or a fine of one thousand dollars.

A Wake-up Call

Judge Hart gave my father the minimum sentence: thirty days of unsupervised probation. The judge's words that day still stand out for me like bright white against a blue sky: "It does sound to me that Mr. Dent was more of an innocent victim than the perpetrator."[5]

From the back of the room, grasping only that Dad had been pronounced guilty, Mom slumped and wept. Dad shouldered his way through the crowd to be with my mother and explained to her that the judge's sentence and remarks were laced with generosity and regard. Dad always brought out the best in people, which must have had some effect on the judge that day. However, no one in our family really credited that afternoon's pronouncement to Dad's charm. Years later we all had the humility to understand that it was only by God's grace that he was set free.

Even now the irony of Dad's disgrace brings tears to my eyes. Haldeman's clearing the White House of my father eventually cleared my father of association with all the Nixon White House covert activity. That shame ultimately saved him. Out of twenty-seven indicted White House appointees, Harry Dent was one of two men to avoid prison sentences. The other was Henry Kissinger. Yet even in that moment Dad knew, as we all did, that as the ship was going down, God had thrown him a life preserver.

Who knew an entire family could hold its breath for so long? Dad left the courtroom to call me at school, and I remember standing, holding the phone receiver as he talked a mile a minute. I practically skipped from the dorm to pick up Jack at football practice; as I waited on the sidelines, taking in the end of my brother's scrimmage, I was undone by God's goodness. There was no need ever to tell Jack that his dad was going to prison. In a single afternoon, this turn of affairs was like getting an "A" on four years' worth of college exams, buying the matching lottery ticket, falling in love, dancing the night away and hearing that a lump was benign. The Dents were free. We could laugh and dance again. Dad joked that his unsupervised probation made Mom liable to seeing that he was a good boy. It was surreal how God had answered our prayers in such a miraculous way.

"Bless you, prison," Alexander Solzhenitsyn famously said in his astonishing address to the 1978 Harvard graduating class. "I nourished my soul there, and I say without hesitation, 'Bless you, prison, for having been in my life.'" In a similar way my dad was thankful for the Watergate experience. In our family's dark era, I had been gripped by fear, always afraid that at any moment everything, everyone that mattered to me would be taken. Now I knew pure release and abject gratitude.

It was a wake-up call. Coming so close to a prison sentence, so close to seeing an entire livelihood rescinded, causes a person to reevaluate priorities. Dad said little after the ordeal, but within him something important was shifting. More discernibly, in all of us, new compassion took permanent bloom. We were quick to help any person or family going through its own type of Watergate. My father had yet to surrender to God, but an awareness of "More than me, more than now" was showing up in his table prayers and far exceeded "Thanks for the food, amen."

The Other Court

In that media-packed federal room, Dad also began to stand taller in the public court, where reactions came in two extremes.

In a radio segment he called "Jury System Indicted," an infuriated Paul Harvey scolded the US courts. "Harry Dent was set free, but our legal system was indicted. Washington's best legal brains agree there was no wrongdoing—Mr. Dent is not accused of stealing anything, hurting anyone, or handling any of the money. But they also agreed that for Dent to face trial in Watergate-conscious Washington would be political suicide," Harvey said.[6]

Our home-state papers had always assumed the best. "A South Carolinian whose integrity we trust has suffered unjust embarrassment in a Washington court," ran an editorial in The *Charleston Evening Post*. "As a longtime admirer of Harry Dent, who ably served as a voice for the South in the White House, we sympathize with his plight and defend his reputation for truth and honesty. In a sense that we deeply deplore, American Justice was the loser in this unfair prosecution of a worthy citizen."[7]

Leaving it to other newspapers to support Harry Dent, the *Washington Post* would hold to its own slant, attempting to connect my father with Watergate and its shame for the rest of his life. Still, Jack Anderson of the *Washington Post* admitted in his column in November 1974, "Dent is personally regarded as honest, even by his enemies."[8] And of course his own party supported him. On December 16, at a Republican fundraiser in Columbia, Dad received a standing ovation from the partisan crowd.

Deep Throat

Deep Throat is the pseudonym the media gave to the secret informant who provided information to *Washington Post* reporters Bob Woodard and Carl Bernstein. The two men vowed to protect their source until after he died, but that stopped no one from guessing.

For years, experts and amateurs speculated about the identity of Deep Throat. *People* magazine and a "Watergate Twentieth Anniversary Special" on *CBS News* both pointed to Pat Gray, the FBI director who succeeded J. Edgar Hoover. William Sullivan, an FBI assistant director, and Henry Peterson, head of the Justice Department Criminal Division, were also chief suspects. A book called *Silent Coup* pegged General Al Haig as the mystery man, believing he had the right combination of access and motive. Almost every White House insider from Chuck Colson to Robert Finch to Fred Fielding to Leonard Garment to my dear sweet dad was in the rumor mill.

Richard Whalen, a distinguished historian and journalist, felt strongly that Deep Throat was a staffer in the Nixon White House—someone like Robert Finch, a disappointed liberal, or my dad, a Southern conservative with a reputation for integrity.[9] He also profiled Deep Throat as an idealist wanting revenge against the Haldeman-Ehrlichman "beaver patrol" of clean-cut, flat-topped lieutenants. This beaver patrol was a group of arm twisters that kept the entire White House under their thumbs. Keep in mind, however, that Bob Woodward, in his Watergate bestseller *All the President's Men*, had sketched his shadow source as a scotch-drinking cigarette smoker—which is why any reference to my father made me laugh.

Years later, in 2005, one blog that pinned Dad as the mystery man had a few things right: It said Dent was one of only a few aides who had by bypassed prison, though he was privy to the "inner circle of the White House, and he retreated from public eye after Watergate."[10]

Fair enough. Dad did have inside access—until Haldeman bumped him out. Dad left Washington right about the time of Watergate, and he was unhappy with some goings-on. And true, he had disliked Haldeman and Ehrlichman's beaver patrol. But the deal killer is that Dad had no need for revenge—that and the fact that he was no squealer. The most disqualifying facts, however, were the descriptions of Deep Throat's bad habits—scotch and tobacco—and my father's avoidance of one and disgust for the other. Dad's alcoholic father had drunk and smoked incessantly. Enough said.

One of the greatest conspiracy puzzles of the political world was finally solved in 2005 when Mark Felt revealed in a *Vanity Fair* article that he had been Deep Throat. Felt, then an assistant director of the FBI, had expected to take Hoover's place as director upon Hoover's death, but had been passed over when Nixon appointed Gray instead. So there was the revenge element. Despite all the scotch and cigarettes, he lived to be ninety-five.

Lessons from Watergate

What had Watergate taught us? In the broadest sense, it brought home in many ways that no one is above the law: no woman, no man and no president. Within that principle Watergate brought on an avalanche of specific lessons, the first being that we reap what we sow. (My father grieved on January 1, 1975, when attorney John Mitchell became the only US attorney general to ever be incarcerated in the prison system he was sworn to oversee.) Another truth Watergate brought to light is that with God's help, redemption can reach to any depth—as witnessed by Chuck Colson's walking out of prison to become a modern-day prophet.

Had he been honest with the American people, Richard Nixon's outcome might have borne its own stamp of redemption. Dad believed that without Watergate, Nixon would have entered history close to Washington and Lincoln in popularity. He also fully believed that Nixon could have stayed in office if he had only fessed up. Initially unaware of the break-in or the massive cover-up, Dad at first refused to believe that his boss would order either. Information later came out that suggested Nixon himself had possibly ordered the break-in.

It wasn't until April of 1977, during his interview with David Frost, that Nixon finally gave his confession on live TV. In his own words:

> I brought myself down. I gave them a sword and they stuck it in and twisted it with relish. I would have done the same thing in their position. I let down my friends, my country. I let the American people down, and I have to carry that burden for the rest of my life. . . . It is true, I made mistakes, my political life is over. I made so many bad judgments, mistakes of the heart rather than the head. If one is to lead, the head must always rule the heart.

But the most revealing thing Nixon said to Frost was, "When the president does it—that means it's not illegal." My dad, sadly, was proven wrong in his estimation of the president.

It is no secret that earlier administrations also engaged in wiretaps and breaking and entering. Nixon tried to justify himself by pointing to the wrongdoings of previous administrations, highlighting a third important lesson: two wrongs don't make a right. History is a lens through which we look; it is hardly a moral compass.[11]

A verse comes to mind from the apostle Paul's first letter to the Corinthians: "God chose the foolish things of the world to shame the wise; God chose the weak things of the world to shame the strong" (1:27). We witnessed that from front-row seats.

The final lesson of Watergate is that Americans can do no less than hold high officials to high standards—and the same goes for media. Unless "righteousness" and "truth" are a package deal, one can't uphold the system of checks and balances that is vital to a free society. Today's descendants of the media sentinels who labored away undoing the Watergate deception must scrutinize every administration (Democrat or Republican), or else they give up the high standards we stand for.

The Correct Footnote for History

For most journalists Harry S. Dent is a footnote in a sinister chapter in national politics, and for most historians my father's story ends at that annotation. When my dad died, decades after Watergate, the *Washington Post* and the *New York Times* both ran obituaries of him, and both mentioned the Townhouse Operation and Dad's guilty plea. It was as though Watergate was what defined his life. I would say, and I hope this book proves, that Watergate was just the beginning of Harry Dent's life. After Watergate he was just catching his second wind.

Senate Chaplain Richard C. Halverson wrote the foreword to my father's autobiography. "It was his own Watergate that prompted Harry to begin a search for the real truth," Halverson wrote. The religious conversion of Watergate co-conspirator Chuck Colson would later fuel the spark that kindled my father's conversion. As with Colson, my father's new birth is all the more interesting because of its stark contrast to his prior life.

The life that unfolded after Watergate is more remarkable that the life before, from a daughter's-eye view.

9

FORBIDDEN KNOWLEDGE AND PATH

After my sophomore year at Columbia College, I found that psychology didn't have all the answers to life in and of itself. I really wanted to go to Columbia Bible College (CIU), but my father forbade me to go there. He considered it a dead-end road to success. He even invited Dr. Ed Young, then pastor of First Baptist Columbia which I was attending, to our house for dinner, hoping my own pastor would convince me that Baylor University was a great place for me to go. I suggested Wheaton as a compromise. Finally, my dad allowed me to go to Wheaton only because in his eyes it was the lesser of two evils. I transferred to Chicago's Wheaton College (the alma mater of Billy Graham) for the summer term of 1975, where I felt I could get an integration of the Bible and psychology.

My first day in the "Windy City" was interesting, to say the least. After getting settled in, I found out that my roommate wasn't the one I had requested. But I believe that the Lord brought a different roommate to me for a reason. She was a fun-loving, petite girl. The first time we met, we spent most of the day together. We went out to eat and saw a movie. She asked me why I had come to Wheaton all the way from South Carolina. I told her I was there to study psychology and Bible. Then she asked me if I could help her. It tuned out that she was depressed and had already attempted suicide once. I tried as best I could to help her see that her heavenly Father was someone who loved her and had a beautiful plan for her life. God was once again revealing to me my calling.

At Wheaton College I was fortunate enough to meet a mature Christian couple who unselfishly took me under their wings. The Lord had not blessed them with children of their own, and as a result, they were like surrogate parents to many students. They gave spiritual counsel to as many as thirty young people, many of whom didn't have a father in their lives. I had a wonderful father, but he wasn't a spiritual leader at that time. I see now that Joan and Alden Nickerson were part of God's plan for my life. They were the spiritual parents I needed. I call them my adopted spiritual parents, and they are a part of my life even today.

After being at Wheaton College for a semester, I felt an even stronger leading to study Bible at CIU, where I felt I could get a stronger biblical foundation before studying psychology. Several wise Christians, including Buck Hatch who taught at CIU, advised me to do this since I hadn't been taught the Bible in a systematic manner growing up. So back to my father I went to persuade him that CIU was where I needed to be.

After several long conversations, Dad gave his halfhearted consent, saying he didn't like it and that I would never be a success in this world. But he didn't (wouldn't) stop me. I had worked all summer at Hilton Head Island waiting tables, baby-sitting, and even cleaning houses and condos to save up enough money to pay my own tuition, room and board if I needed to. My father had forgotten how hardheaded, independent and stubborn I could be—and why he had given me the nickname "Sassy Pooh-pooh" when I was growing up. But now he was beginning to see that this apple had not fallen far from the tree.

Money Can't Buy Me Love

Being away at Wheaton College made me realize something else. Although I had always been a very self-sufficient person, I discovered that my life wasn't as complete without a very special someone whom I had left behind in Columbia. Absence had indeed made my heart grow fonder of my former high-school boyfriend. I had broken up with him, but over time the Lord had answered my prayers and begun working in Alton's heart.

The first time I had seen Alton was at a high-school basketball game during my sophomore year. My giggly girlfriends and I were watching him and talking about him, as girls will do. (And we thought guys were bad about talking about girls!) Since we were discussing how cute he was, we were horrified when a nearby girl told us that his parents were sitting right in front of us! My face turned five shades of red. Then she said, "Don't worry; they can't hear you. They're deaf." Then this girl went on to tell me how much Alton looked out for his parents and how much he loved them. That impressed me even more. At that time, most of the guys I knew were rebelling against their parents. Character was always the number one thing that attracted me to a person, especially someone I thought I might marry one day.

My father wasn't too fond of Alton and his background, for he wanted to make sure his little princess was well taken care of. He tried to turn my head to more affluent guys, but if they didn't have true character, I wasn't interested. I can remember one particular guy in Washington DC who took me out for dinner and tried to make an impression with his family fortune, his jaguar and the sculptured ice swan that he had arranged to be brought to our table. Any guy who tried to capture my attention with such things automatically flunked my test.

But with Alton I was immediately impressed with his determination, his perseverance, his respect for his parents and his great personality. I wanted someone who would be a good father and a hard worker and who would be humble, caring and understanding. I also wanted a man who would one day be the spiritual leader of my family—someone whose purpose in life was more than making money.

I ran into Alton several months after he made his commitment to the Lord, and we began dating again. As the Lord continued working in his life, I recognized the kind of man I had always wanted. Alton had given up his business major at the University of South Carolina to study Bible at CIU, which I admired. But when he did this, my dad told him he would never have my hand in marriage. This is how my father put it in his autobiography:

> On returning from the Presidential Prayer Breakfast, I encountered a problem with Ginny, the third of our four children. She had experienced this born-again phenomenon as a member of Young Life, a ministry to high school students. Ginny had infected her boyfriend, Alton Brant, with this contagion.
>
> Earlier, I had tried to end their romance because he was the son of deaf parents. Alton was a nice young fellow, but he did not represent my idea of a "SUCCESSFUL" son-in-law. He was working his way through the University of South Carolina by tarring roofs and working other odd jobs. And now he was too religious. This born-again thing made him sound crazy to me. He would talk about "The Word." Finally, I asked, "What word are you talking about?" He responded, "God's Word!" Then I said, "But God's got lotsa words, doesn't he?"
>
> Ginny wanted to transfer from what I considered a normal Christian college to an "abnormal" one, Columbia International University. Her fanatical boyfriend was behind this desire, so I told her to bring him to our home to discuss the matter.
>
> Ginny brought him. I will never forget our conversation, for it was quite an experience for me. For two hours I informed Alton that he could never be a success if he transferred to Columbia International University. I picked apart the curriculum as having too much religion and not enough business courses. I suggested that he get his business degree from the university and give 10% of his income to God's work.
>
> At the end of the one-sided dialogue, I then delivered this solemn warning, "If you go to that Bible college and Ginny follows you, you will never have the hand of my daughter in holy

matrimony!" All I could remember Alton saying was "But Mr. Dent; but Mr. Dent; but Mr. Dent."

Ginny was a model and a beauty contestant. Yet, Alton walked out of my den that day with an impressive Christian demeanor. He was nice as he departed, and I thought I had prevailed. But he went straight to Columbia International University and risked his "second love" Ginny. He was listening to the beat of a different drummer, his heavenly Father, his first love. This left me every bit perplexed as the Chuck Colson prayer breakfast meeting had. Later he told me, "Mr. Dent, I could never leave Ginny, no matter what. It's not just because I love her. You see, Mr. Dent, she led me to my Lord." Later I gave in to their wedding plans.[1]

My decision to go to Columbia International University that fall was the hardest one I ever made. Although my father allowed it, my choice did not please him. I cried the whole way to CIU; I needed windshield wipers on my eyes more than on my poor car. I was driving my 1960 Chevy Nova, complete with peeling paint. My father felt it would be a good car for me since I would be living the rest of my life in poverty due to this decision.

There was no one I loved and wanted to please more on this earth than my daddy. After all, I was a daddy's girl. There was a tug of war in my heart, and it was splitting me apart. I was torn between my earthly father, who had lovingly held me in his arms and clapped when I took my first steps, and my heavenly Father, who had formed me in my mother's womb, knew me better than I knew myself and had prepared the best-made plan for my life.

It was no contest. I knew I must follow the leading of my heavenly Father. But it isn't easy saying no to a father who has advised presidents and who seems to know it all. In the midst of my tears that day, this special verse from Matthew 6:33 came to mind, and it has become my life verse: "Seek first his kingdom and his righteousness, and all these things will be given to you as well." Suddenly a total peace came over me, as if God was saying, "Do as I have led you, and I will take care of these other things that are troubling you." This peace that God would take care of my relationship with my dad gave me the confidence to know that I was doing the right thing, no matter how difficult the right thing was to do. And it was a promise I would one day see fulfilled over and above my expectations.

A Marriage Ordained in Heaven . . . for Two Church Mice

Alton and I were married on December 20, 1975, after having dated on and off for five years. We waited on my father's approval, and he finally consented, admitting, "Alton is one of the finest young men I have ever met." Alton's hard work and determination reminded Dad of his own college years, when he too had worked himself through school amidst negative circumstances.

In one of the most unusual ceremonies held in Columbia, we gave our vows in voice and in sign language, and we dedicated our marriage to our Lord and Savior with our own prayer at the end. Nearly one thousand people attended the wedding. Present there were deaf people from all over the state as well as governors, senators and congressmen. Dr. Raymond Scott of Columbia International University performed the ceremony.

One wedding gift from my father included a painting of a shack in the woods. It was his subtle reminder that with the road we were taking, we would be nothing more than poor church mice, nibbling cheese and living in a shack for the rest of our lives. Thanks for the word of encouragement, Dad!

10

JUST CAN'T GIVE IT UP

Once my father started working part time from our home in South Carolina in 1972, he promised my mother that he would not spend so much time away attending to political issues. But promises made can be hard to keep when politics runs through your every vein. It can be as hard as separating an addict from his cocaine.

Back in October 1973, when Spiro Agnew had been forced to step down from the office of vice president, Gerald Ford had been appointed to the position by President Nixon. After Nixon resigned, this unelected vice president became our new president. *Integrity* was the one word that summed up this giant of a man, who was confirmed quite easily. America was disillusioned with the Republicans after Watergate, and Ford was just what this country needed.

My father knew Nixon had hoped that John Connally of Texas would succeed him as the next Republican president. My father had been in charge of Connally's nomination for Secretary of the Treasury in 1971. He was amazed when, the night before his confirmation hearings, John Connally asked my father to provide all the treasury budget documents. My dad actually hand rolled carts of documents to Connally's hotel room, and the former Texas governor stayed up all night reading them. Connally knocked the ball out of the park during the confirmation hearings the next day, securing his appointment. After that experience my father grew to admire this tall Texan whose brilliance had shown during those hearings. John Connally became known as "Big John" to the Nixon Administration and was particularly liked by the president.

But Connally, while serving as Secretary of the Treasury under Nixon's administration, had switched from the Democratic Party to the Republican in May 1973. When Nixon had to choose a replacement for Spiro Agnew five months later, Connally was initially his choice, but he veered at the last minute to Gerald Ford, knowing that the Democrats would devour a man who had abandoned their party.

Following Nixon's resignation in 1974, Gerald Ford served the presidency well and proved that Nixon had made a wise choice. My father continued his part-time, long-distance political work by serving in an advisory role for the new president. When Ford decided that he wanted to continue in his role as commander in chief and seek the 1976 Republican nomination for president, my father ran his campaign and worked hard to help him win. President Ford himself said, "Harry Dent went the extra mile for me in contributing to my nomination of the Republican Party in 1976. His greatest political contribution has been working with other leaders to bring the South back into the mainstream of modern American politics. He is one of America's foremost political strategists and experts on southern politics in this day."[1]

It was a tough battle behind the scenes as delegates wavered between Ronald Reagan and Gerald Ford for the Republican nomination. No delegation was more wooed and pressured at the 1976 GOP convention than Mississippi's uncommitted thirty delegates. My father's advice to Ronald Reagan was clear: "Don't go to the far right of Goldwater." In other words, Goldwater's extreme conservatism had lost him the 1964 election, and my dad felt a more balanced approach would be more acceptable. Again, Dad's love for Reagan was tough to put aside, but he secretly hoped that Ford would win, and that Reagan would be Ford's vice-presidential selection.

In the end, the Mississippi delegation went with Ford after flip-flopping between the two candidates. Ford was nominated by a vote of 1187 to 1070. My father was disappointed when Ford chose Senator Robert Dole over Reagan as his running mate. He had great respect for Senator Dole and his wife Elizabeth—but he simply wanted Reagan in that spot.

In the presidential race it was clear that the country was still reeling from the Watergate scandal. They were ready for a new face. Ford lost the election to Jimmy Carter.

The main reason the GOP lost the White House, probably, was because Ford pardoned Richard Nixon, which produced a political backlash. Ford was convinced that it was the right thing to do; he never backed down from that and emphatically said he would have done it again if given the opportunity. Another contributor to the GOP's loss was their failure to unite sooner in the primaries. The hotly contested race between Ford and Reagan helped cause their defeat. The Democrats would have the same trouble four years later when Ted Kennedy challenged the Democratic incumbent Carter, and cold stares between the two cast a dark cloud on their convention in 1982.

Ford was dedicated to maintaining freedom, justice and equality for all. Although his pardoning of Nixon was unpopular, Ford believed several men from the Watergate period were honorable men and were just caught up in the political and litigious firestorm that came from the scandal. In an effort to give a few of them back their good names, he appointed them to presidential commissions. My father was one of those men.[2]

It's too bad Ford didn't have more time to implement his policies. The peace and stability he brought after the storm of Watergate will never be forgotten. He was a great man who held this nation together during a time of political unrest.

Another Avenue of Service

My father was a gentleman and a visionary. Besides his hard work politically to invest in our country, he used his law practice to help numerous individuals and organizations, and he did this for little or no monetary gain. In fact, out of love for my husband and his parents, he helped the deaf community of South Carolina in three extraordinary ways.

First, in 1977, Mrs. Nelda Barnes of Spartanburg was a deaf teacher at the South Carolina School for the Deaf (SCAD). She was working on recertifying her teaching certificate and applied to attend Converse College. She was denied admission to the college because they didn't want to provide an interpreter for her. Nelda filed a complaint in the fourth circuit court and won access to the classroom. The officials at Converse College were forced to provide her an interpreter. One of the attorneys representing Mrs. Barnes was my father. The Barnes Case was a landmark decision not only in South Carolina, but also throughout the US. Deaf and hearing impaired children now have access to classrooms via interpreters because of this significant court decision.

Second, during the late 1970s, a number of people within the deaf community asked that the South Carolina School for the Deaf and the Blind (SCSDB) appoint one of the seats on the board of trustees to a deaf person. Up until that time, no deaf person had served on the SCSDB board overseeing the management of the school. My dad found out about the lack of representation on the board and called the president of the school, Dr. A. Baron Holmes. He convinced Dr. Holmes that having a deaf representative on the board was in the "best interest" of SCSDB. With the next vacancy on the SDSDB board, Mr. Harry Culpepper, a deaf man from Belton, was appointed. He served for twenty-eight years.

And third, also in the late 1970s, there was a movement in the South Carolina deaf community to establish a commission for the deaf in the South Carolina government. There had been several attempts to establish a commission in the past, but they had all been unsuccessful. In 1979, at the convention for SCAD, my father got Democratic Governor Dick Riley (who later became the secretary of education for the US) to address the association. To my knowledge, this was the first and only time a governor has ever attended and addressed such a convention. He promised the deaf community that he would do all he could to establish a "voice" for the deaf in state government. Governor Riley got the ball rolling, and in 1982 the SCAD home office was established. We have always appreciated what my father and Governor Riley together did to help the deaf of South Carolina. In Alton's and my opinion, this was politics at its finest—two men from opposing parties working together to help those who really needed it.

Staying in Control

My father always wanted to be in control, but in a good way. He liked to use his influence sacrificially to help other people get ahead. He helped Senator Thurmond get elected, he helped Nixon get elected, and he helped Ford get nominated. It was part of his generous spirit.

Even in his law practice my dad was generous. During my college years I worked part time in his law office. When I realized how much of his time was spent helping political candidates at his own expense and how many clients he didn't charge, I was taken aback. I often wondered how he made a living.

His administrative assistant and I spoke of it often. We would joke about which of us should tell him he needed to charge some clients so we could pay the bills. My good-hearted father was in some ways a "Robin Hood" lawyer. He didn't steal from the rich—he just charged them the fair amount—but he certainly gave to the poor. He was good about not charging those who couldn't afford to pay or who had been taken advantage of. Harry Dent was always out for a good cause. It did not take me long to realize that my dad's law office was just a front for his political activities and his desire to help folks who were in need.

This is one way in which Dad was like a Democrat—always involving himself with social concerns. He did what he felt was right, and he did it from his heart. Government service and law never provided my dad with much money. He made his income through wise investments in real estate and in an automobile dealership, and just kept on trying to do good.

Because he loved helping others, it was hard for my dad to give up his political addiction. My mother never liked politics—she saw it as an ego trip, and she was right. I always saw it as scheming to make the world fit into what one thinks is right. But it had its hold on my dad. It's not that politics in and of itself is bad; my dad just did not know where to draw the line between politics and family. Money, materialism, fame, sports or alcohol and drugs can also become idols or addictions that consume our lives. For my dad, the idol was politics.

While the American two-party system isn't perfect, the checks and balances that the parties and the Constitution offer help keep us on an even keel. It is the behind-the-scenes wrangling that is so important to getting things done, and my father fought hard for the right things in Washington. It is this background process that keeps our American democracy what it is. A viable two-party system is an important component of a democracy, because if one party rules without checks or balances, we can end up in a socialized democracy. My father fought hard for freedom because he never wanted to see that happen.

This is the reason politics still had its hold on him. Dad was convinced he could control the direction of the country that he loved with all his heart. I wanted to tell him that God controls the entire world. I wanted to tell him that good works could not get him into heaven. I wanted him to realize that politics does not determine one's mission in life, God does. But as Buck Hatch had advised me, I continued to keep my thoughts to myself.

There is a place for standing for the freedoms of this country.

We are fortunate that we live in a country where we can stand for what we believe to be right—but my dad simply had his priorities out of balance. Harry Dent, known to all as a God-and-country man, was a good man with good intentions.

Dad was still trying to control the destiny of his country with one hand—and his daughter with the other. And Alton and I continued to pray for the Lord to work in my father's heart. We had high hopes that he would one day see that God was more than a force for moral good.

11

THE
FINAL
SURRENDER

After our honeymoon, Alton and I returned to the real world. We were two full-time students, newly married and working our way through CIU. Although my father had never wanted me to attend CIU and initially refused to pay for it, after we were married he generously offered to support us through college. Alton had a lot of pride, though, and felt we couldn't be a Christian witness to my father if we lived off him, so he turned down the offer. Finally, after much persuasion, Alton agreed to let my father pay for my tuition, at least, since my dad felt it was his responsibility to do that for each of his children. From there, we would have to make it on our own.

Though we had some tough financial times—the result of a $350 a month income for more than three years—our marriage grew and prospered, as did our spiritual lives. We learned from the beginning of our marriage to tithe, no matter what we did or did not have—and to depend upon God.

The training at CIU was invaluable. To begin our lives studying God's Word together greatly benefited our marriage and the raising of our children. The courses we took included Old and New Testament, marriage and family, child psychology and other subjects from a Christian point of view. They started us out on the right foot and enabled us to avoid many mistakes we might have otherwise made.

Our deep happiness and commitment during those tough financial and stressful times puzzled my father. He watched many of my peers going through divorce even though they had been married under the best of circumstances. And here we were prospering spiritually even though we had been married under the worst of circumstances (being full-time students and from differing backgrounds). Although Alton and I had come from dissimilar circumstances, our hearts and our goals were the same, and Christ was the center of our marriage. My father started seeing what a difference that could make.

One day Dad came to our small house to find something, and he was snooping to make sure we were making it financially. He saw my Bible on my nightstand with a prayer list on top. And guess whose name was first on the list?

He wrote about that moment in his autobiography:

> After they were married and were students at CBC [CIU], Betty and I went to their apartment to get something from them. They were out so I went looking for the object. Over their bed I spied a written prayer list. I laughed and called Betty to come see it. I said, "Have you ever seen anything like this before?" Then my laughter stopped when Betty read off the name at the top. It was DADDY. In addition to praying me into God's Kingdom, they were also praying me through Watergate. Since then in giving my testimony, I have sometimes been introduced by young adults who said their prayer group had been praying for me at the request of Ginny and Alton.[1]

As I prayed for my dad, God began pulling and tugging at his heart, even though I didn't know it. There were times when I was discouraged at not seeing results. I wondered if I would ever see the day when my father and I would share a biblical worldview. *Would we ever dance to the same tune again?* What I did not realize during those five to six years of praying for my dad was that God had been answering my prayers from the moment I uttered my first helpless words. Yes, God was not being silent; He had been working the entire time.

There were several key factors to my dad's conversion. Not only did God work in his life through our prayers; He also used the scandal of Watergate to shake Dad from his pew. Watergate was a strain on all of us for several years, but God used it in our lives for good. My father realized that had he not been removed from the inner circle of the White House several months before Watergate was planned, he could have been indicted as part of the cover-up, which would have assuredly meant prison time. His resistance to hardball politics gave him a reputation as a softy and as someone who was unreliable for covert missions.[2] In retrospect, he knew that our prayers were integral in his being spared time in prison. Deep inside, he knew God had rescued him.

Another important factor in my dad's conversion was the conversion of Chuck Colson. Several years after Colson appeared at the White House prayer meeting in 1973 to give his testimony, my father told him, "Chuck, I'm convinced your born-again experience is for real. Watergate is the best thing that ever happened to you."[3] And Chuck agreed. My father clearly saw the change in Colson's life, and it had a direct effect on him. Alton and I had been praying that God would bring people into Dad's life who would influence him.

My dear sweet mom was also pointing my father toward God as best she could, but she still needed God to heal her own soul. My specific prayer for that was answered when a Christian businessman and his wife, Jack and Betty Matthews, moved down the street from my parents and shared the gospel with them.

But my father claims that the people who had the biggest influence on his life were my husband (whom he affectionately called "the ghetto kid"), because of Alton's heart and character, and me, the shy little girl who he and my mom worried about the most when I was growing up. My father, by the way, had finally acknowledged that Alton was the best son-in-law any man could have. After that, I never wanted to consider what my dad would do if he ever had to choose between my husband and me.

Too Close for Comfort

There is nothing like a traumatic event in a loved one's life to bring you to your knees. We thought we had been through the worst with Watergate, but the possible loss of a loved one is the toughest trial one can face. About one year after Alton and I married, my beautiful sister Dolly was playing racquetball one day with a college student who worked part time at a hospital. Within twenty-four hours of the game, her temperature reached an alarming 105 degrees, and she had excruciating pain in her head and back. My parents called our family doctor, John Rider. Since it was Thanksgiving Day, he told Dad to take Dolly to the emergency room. By the time they arrived at Palmetto Baptist Hospital, his eldest daughter, whom he affectionately called Dolly Dumplings, was turning gray and slipping into a coma.

The doctors were puzzled. My parents sat next to her bed, knowing she might not make it—and the worst part was that they didn't know why. Finally, when a medical student friend of my sister's found out she was in the emergency room, he came by to make sure the doctors knew that she may have been exposed to bacterial meningitis. That racquetball game had passed more than a few balls to my sister: the student she had been playing with had been exposed to the disease through a child at the hospital. My sister was twenty-two years old, and at the time, people thought it was highly unlikely that an adult could get bacterial meningitis. It was mainly known as a children's disease then. But after a spinal tap was done, the diagnosis of bacterial spinal meningitis was certain. The doctors immediately began to give her penicillin intravenously. We were left to wait for days.

Dolly hung between life and death, and she lay motionless in her own world. I had rarely seen my father cry, but now he wept for his daughter. His children meant everything to him, and he fell down on his knees begging God to save her.

It was days before we would see Dolly awaken from the coma. For a while she had double vision, difficulty keeping her balance and deafness in one ear. But she was growing a little better day by day. Eventually her vision improved and her balance was restored. Weak and frail, we were warned that she might have complications the rest of her life; God's grace, however, was poured out on us. The only complication from her meningitis was that she remained deaf in that one ear—and we were all grateful that's all she had to live with. Now my sister always warns me as we walk down the beach to "walk on my right side—not the left." It was a small price to pay, considering how close she came to dying.

In my opinion, this incident became the straw that broke the camel's back for my father. In my mind I could hear him saying, "Put me in prison . . . take away everything I have, but Lord, please don't take my precious baby girl." But we were spared. There was no mistaking it; God had thrown us a life preserver once again.

Walking Where Jesus Walked

My mother got just what she wanted for her twenty-fifth wedding anniversary in January of 1977: she convinced my ever-working father to stop practicing law for a few weeks and take her to the Holy Land with a Columbia pastor, Dr. Ed Young. Reluctantly, he agreed. It turned out to be the trip of a lifetime for both of them. I'll never forget my father calling Alton and me at two in the morning upon his return to say, "It's all really true, Ginny and Alton. I walked where Jesus walked, and it all really happened."

We did not have to go on that trip to know that Jesus was real. But what it did for my dad was unbelievable. Finally, God had my father's heart in His hands, and He was changing him day by day. My dad hadn't taken a final step of faith, but his thirst to read the Bible and his eager questions kept us on our toes.

From Political to Spiritual Evangelist

In February 1978 my father finally gave his life to God. He realized that nothing he had done would make him righteous in God's eyes. He had started Senate and White House prayer breakfasts; he had been featured in *Time* magazine as the good guy who did not smoke, drink, cuss, chew or chase any woman but his own wife; he had been a church member in good standing since the age of thirteen and even been a deacon and a Sunday school teacher. But none of these things made him righteous. No, Harry Dent was not a righteous man—he was a self-righteous man.

In his own words:

> On a Monday morning in February, 1978, I abdicated the throne of my life to Jesus Christ. There was rain inside the car as well as outside as I prayed with misty eyes all the one hundred miles to Greenville, SC. I had made promises to Him so many times before. However, I had never really followed through with a heart and life commitment as Paul calls for in Romans 12:1–2. On this Monday morning, I realized this meant surrender of my determined will to live no longer by Harry's law, but by God's law. This was going to require more in worship, commitment and work from me. I remembered the Bible teachings promise the Holy Spirit would help as my "Special Counsel."
>
> I knew this would last forever. I had come to understand the difference between finite and infinite, between today and forever, between man's hidden agendas and God's open agenda. I felt truly free for the first time in my life. Freedom is what I had wanted all my life, but I wanted to be free to do everything my way. Now I would have a Chairman of my board to help me make the decisions of life. Surrendering this self-control for supernatural guidance turned out to be the best deal I have ever struck, and it was God's grace, not my work. I had finally appropriated that gift by accepting the Giver as my Lord and Savior. I promised God I would no longer be part of the problems in this world, but part of the solution.[4]

The change in my father's heart was something my mother had always longed for. After trying to be the spiritual leader of our family for nearly twenty years and attending churches that didn't teach the Bible, many times she had been left hopeless and in despair. Now she was overjoyed by Dad's transformation.

You might say my father was having a midlife crisis. Although he had achieved success in law, politics and business, he had always focused on his worldly accomplishments and neglected his spiritual life. At age forty-eight he finally realized he didn't have unlimited time left on this earth, and it caused him to think about what he had done in his life that really mattered. But instead of buying a sports car or running after younger women, he ran hard and fast after God's will for his life. I wish more men and women would have a midlife crisis like my father did.

Alton and I enjoyed every minute of it—especially when Dad left his law practice to attend Columbia International University, the very school he had once forbidden me to attend. Chuck Colson wisely recommended that he get one year of in-depth training before he set out on his new mission in life. Hard to believe that the man the *New York Times* hailed as "one who drinks and smokes nothing but politics" was now hungering and thirsting on every word from Genesis to Revelation.[5]

During his Nixon years my father had actually been quoted, on April 22, 1972, as saying, "Like the Bible, we are going from Genesis to Revelation and showing the president as a man of peace."[6] At that time my father was hailed as the "Nixon Evangelist" who went out to sell what the president was doing and saying. Now, in his new life, he would learn the true meaning of all God's wisdom from Genesis to Revelation, which was something he had mistakenly thought he already knew. Now he would become an evangelist for the only true God. And instead of my father being the one to manipulate circumstances and minds, he would see that God alone controlled his life and the fate of the entire world.

Do you remember that picture my father gave me when we got married? The painting of that shack in the woods? Of course my husband and I couldn't resist the urge to make light of the irony of it all. We gave Dad all the reasons why he shouldn't go to CIU—that he would never be a success in this world and that he would be a poor church mouse who nibbled at cheese. And we gave him back the shack picture as a reminder.

After seeing the change in my father's life, my sister eventually rededicated her life to the Lord and has been serving Him ever since. My younger brother, whom I had helped care for during my high-school years, also gave his life to Christ. This shows what happens when a man becomes the spiritual leader of his family.

Yes, at age forty-eight, my father gave his heart and his life to our Lord Jesus Christ. He had been caught up in the drive for worldly success, which the Bible clearly warns us against. He tried to infect me with it too. He wholeheartedly admits that politics was his first love and the lord of his life. He was driven to success, trying to overcome his younger days of embarrassment over his own father's alcoholism and failure. He was also trying to make up for the loss of his two beloved brothers, Jack and H.N. Dent, who had been killed in World War II. My dad always checked in with God when he needed Him, but after God had served Harry's purpose, he would always put Him back on hold until he got in another bind.

Alton and I watched the miracle in my father's life after he started listening to the beat of a different Drummer. Some days we were so touched at what God was doing that we cried, and some days we would roar with laughter, amazed at how our Lord had such a sense of humor. To see Dad go back to school as a full-time student in order to learn the Bible from Genesis to Revelation—especially to the forbidden Columbia International University—was more than we had ever dreamed of or prayed for. To see him taught and discipled by the same godly men who made such a difference in our lives—men such as Charlie

Wenzel, Robertson McQuilkin and Buck Hatch—was such a joy to us.

My father had once believed that his greatest day was the one on which he raised his right hand to recite and commit to the oath of office as Special Counsel to the president of the United States. He was to find out that his greatest days were yet ahead. A new life was just beginning at age forty-eight. And my father and I were beginning to dance to the same tune again.

PART TWO

Sharing True Freedom

12

SAME
GIFTS,
NEW LIFE

Now that Dad had given his life to the Lord, his freedom-fighting tendencies took a new turn. He continued his work in politics and in law for several years, but his desires were shifting.

Dad's last political mission was to run George H.W. Bush's primary campaign in South Carolina in 1980. My father greatly admired all three candidates who were running for the Republican ticket—George H.W. Bush, Ronald Reagan and John Connally. When Reagan won the primary in July, my father then put his time and talents behind him. Reagan chose Bush as his vice-presidential running mate, and the ticket was a huge success.

My father, mother and I attended the Reagan-Bush inauguration. It was a wonderful celebration, and the last inauguration we attended.

My dad continued to vote for and to support many godly men who stepped into the political arena, advising them to stand for their faith and for what he believed was best for this country. He did what any decent American citizen should do—nothing more and nothing less. He was appointed to serve on several presidential commissions, and he obliged as an American citizen who wanted to donate his time for the benefit of his country. But in his former life, politics and this country had come first; now my father, a God-and-country man, had finally realized that God and his family had to come before his country.

Senator Thurmond begged Dad several times to come back and run his staff. If my father had worked for Thurmond for two more years, he could have drawn his much-needed federal pension. I can't begin to tell you the many opportunities like that with which he was tempted. Nevertheless, he never returned to law or politics. The pull of these things on my father had finally waned.

Training in the Desert

True success comes from getting away from this world and meeting with God face to face. Jesus Himself often went into the desert to commune with the Father. To know the Lord and to know His thoughts and ways means finding time to know His Word.

My father's "desert" was Columbia International University. He humbly went there to learn everything he could—he wanted to find out what God had to say about life. He enrolled in a one-year graduate degree program in biblical studies for the school year of 1981–82. My dad knew bits and pieces of the Bible—but just enough to twist it to suit his own desires.

That is probably what is wrong with many well-meaning American Christians today who know only bits and pieces of the Bible but who have never understood what God's big picture is all about. For example, my dad thought his good character and morals would get him into heaven, but he came to find that only the blood of Christ can pay for our sins. My mother used to say, "The road to hell is paved with good intentions." Since we had always been a family with good intentions, my father had been leading us, through the lure of worldly success, to the natural destination of those intentions. But now we all knew that God was not interested in our worldly success. He calls us to be faithful first.

Formerly our "big-picture man" in politics, Harry Dent was now reading and ravaging every Christian book and commentary he could put his hands on so he could understand the big picture of the Bible. It was just part of the way God had designed him. It was as if he was starving to digest everything about God and His purpose and His ways.

The professors who had meant so much to Alton and me now became my father's mentors and teachers. Charlie Wenzel, known affectionately to all the students as "Wizzie Wenzel" because he was wise beyond his years, was one of the many godly men who stepped up to the plate to disciple my father. Robertson McQuilkin, the president of the university, became another mentor for my dad, and in the years to come he would be a guiding light to our whole family.

Buck Hatch and his gifts of wisdom and teaching also had a profound influence on both my parents' lives. Alton started picking up my mom, who had persistently continued to seek out a real relationship with God, and took her to sit under Buck's instruction. She was so taken with his gift of teaching that she ended up auditing all his courses. She later told me, "Now I understand why you were so desperate to come to CIU. This is what I have longed for all my life." Nothing helped my mom more than sitting under Buck's teaching. She was finally gaining her own assurance of a relationship with God.

Just being on the campus and interacting with the faculty, staff and students was a wonderful experience for my parents. Dad was known as the "Big Ol' Man on Campus." This was just a nice way of saying that there weren't many men his age (fifty by now) going to school full time. The students took him under their wing and showed him the ropes. He made some very close friendships during that year that he would treasure for the rest of his life.

When my father began feeling led to go into full-time Christian ministry and considered closing his legal and political career, it seemed so drastic that even Robertson McQuilkin questioned whether he was doing the right thing. At fifty years of age, to completely change one's lifestyle can be quite difficult.

And instead of leaving the public square, shouldn't Christians be involved in it?

At that time in my father's life, he had achieved success in law, politics and business. As a result, the hometown boy from St. Matthews, South Carolina, had become a wealthy man by many people's standards. My parents had spent a whole year building a beautiful six-thousand-square-foot home in Spring Valley Country Club, right on the golf course. The circular drive with the water fountain was Dad's pride and joy. The kitchen was my mother's favorite spot. The next thing we knew, my parents were putting a "For Sale" sign out front.

I thought it must have been hard for my dad to convince my mom to give up her pride and joy—her custom-built home. But to my mother, who grew up in poverty, people and ministry were always more important than any possessions. It was a decision they made together. My dad said, "People will not feel that we are for real if we live out here and they cannot see any change in our lives." So they sold their big home on the outskirts of town and built a smaller one closer to Columbia. The new house on Glenwood Court became the gathering place for our family and the home that all my parents' grandchildren would associate as the Dent home place.

Love Means Saying You're Sorry

After his year of study ended, Dad decided to draw his family together for a fireside chat. He had come to realize that for the noble cause of God and country, he had practically deserted his family. During those years of political service, he had thought he was doing the right thing by serving the most important man in the world. My father had three university degrees to prepare him for success—yet he had received no training in marriage or parenting. Now, as he compared the husband and father he had been to what the Bible said he should be, he knew he had fallen short.

With tears in his eyes, my father recounted the many mistakes he had made, including not being home much and not being the spiritual leader of his own family. For these reasons and many more, he made a formal apology to all of us. "I promise to do better by my family," he said. "I only ask for your forgiveness and for you to give me a second chance as your dad."

We all loved our father very much. We knew what he had done in the past, but we also knew that his home and what happened in it were the most important things. There was not a dry eye at the fireside chat that day. We wondered with each new day what changes would come next.

The Southern Strategist Calls It Quits

When my father told us of his decision to close his law practice and go into full-time Christian ministry, my mother was at his side, and we kids were all shocked—and thrilled. The political world lost a great man when the Southern strategist, who had helped to start the modern day Republican Party in the South and helped three Republican presidents get elected, left his legal and political career to enter full-time Christian lay ministry in 1981. A reporter from the *Washington Post* visited our home in Columbia to do an interview about it. She didn't know she was recording a miracle. She was a doubting Thomas who had to touch and feel to believe it for herself.

From the time my father closed his law practice at age fifty, he began working for the Lord. His first few years in ministry were spent working with Columbia International University to help with the development of a new Billy Graham Training Center, known as The Cove.

About ten years previously, the Billy Graham Evangelistic Association (BGEA) had purchased 1,200 acres in the Blue Ridge Mountains near Asheville, North Carolina, with the intention of opening a center for Bible and evangelism training. The BGEA had given this land to CIU for the purpose of developing this center, and when in 1982 Robertson McQuilkin offered my parents an opportunity to oversee the work, it didn't take them long to say yes. So my mom and dad moved again, this time to North Carolina. They lived on the campus of the Ben Lippen college prep Christian school in Asheville, also owned by CIU, while plans for The Cove unfolded. My dad threw himself into his new calling.

There was no one who worked harder to get that project off the ground than my dad. He was so excited that he took my husband, our eighteen-month old son Josh and me all over that property in his new four-wheel-drive Jeep. Dad had been famous for his personal tours of the White House and the Capitol, but there was a distinctive gleam in his eyes when spoke about God's plan for The Cove. My father enjoyed the years he spent working with all the good folks from Ben Lippen and the Billy Graham Association as the first director of the Billy Graham Lay Training Center. This relationship with Billy Graham and his ministry would continue to flourish over the years.

My Father and Billy Graham

My father and Billy Graham go a long way back. When I was just a child, my dad once took our family up to Black Mountain, North Carolina, to visit Dr. and Mrs. Graham. I remember the long winding road that led to the Graham's home perched at the top of the mountain. High barbwire fences surrounded their modest log-cabin home. I never realized until our visit that they had to take many precautions to protect their lives and privacy. They impressed me as being very modest and not overly materialistic. When I would hear someone criticize TV evangelists for their lavish lifestyles and include the Grahams in their generalization, I was always quick to correct them.

The Grahams were gracious hosts. Dr. Graham and my father talked for a long time that day, and I sat there patiently and actually behaved. I will never forget what happened toward the end of our visit that day. When Billy Graham said a word of prayer before we left, I was standing to the left of him, and his German shepherd was seated on his right side. During the prayer the dog came over to sniff me. I have always had a fear of large dogs, especially German shepherds. (My sister and I had an incident with one when we were younger.) Dr. Graham, however, being a kind and observant man, sensed my fear. He stopped right in the middle of his prayer, gave his dog a command in German to back off, and the dog obeyed. He held my hand to make sure I was all right, and then he continued to pray. Ever since then I have stood in awe of him.

It was at the request of Billy Graham that my father started a prayer breakfast in the Nixon White House. Dr. Graham and my father had always had a long-standing friendship, and each respected the other; after the change in my father's life, he became even more involved with the Graham ministries.

Besides having been the first director of The Cove in the early 1980s, my dad would later volunteer, in 1987, to chair the Billy Graham Crusade in Columbia, South Carolina. It was a full-time commitment, beginning about one year before the crusade and continuing about a year afterward. He had many meetings with local churches to get them involved in bringing converts into local churches.

The Graham organization was very thorough and committed to working with the local bodies of believers, and my father and mother were both impressed with the BGEA's cooperative efforts. My parents made many good friends during their time with the crusade. My father would volunteer once again, in 1996, to co-chair the North Carolina-South Carolina Billy Graham Crusade in Charlotte.

Apology for Segregation

In the interview my father had given the *Washington Post* in 1981 to explain why he was leaving politics for full-time ministry, he also apologized to the black community for his early days of standing on the wrong side of civil rights. In looking back on his life and after studying the Beatitudes, he regretted his segregation days.

When he had first worked for Strom Thurmond, he had done his best to thwart the first voting-rights bill—the Civil Rights Act of 1957—a measure which would allow all African Americans the right to vote. In time, however, he proved to be slightly ahead of the curve in promoting the inclusion of African Americans to positions in the White House, in Senator Thurmond's office and in the Republican Party, as well as through his efforts to desegregate public schools in the South.

My father's change of heart was apparent when years later he urged President Ronald Reagan not to weaken the Voting Rights Act of 1982, which had been enacted to restrict states from infringing on the rights of black people to vote. After Dad went into ministry, he often shared in black churches, teaching the Bible and preaching. He wouldn't allow the churches to pay him, and he offered his books as gifts to anyone who wanted them. These were things he felt he needed to do to make amends for his early years in politics when he had supported segregation.

The change in Harry Dent's life was real. When he surrendered his life to Christ, he continued to fight for freedom, but with a new awareness of what freedom truly is. Instead of self-motivated ambition, he was now powered by a love for God and for people. He never looked back.

13

EXPANDING HORIZONS AND NEW OPPORTUNITIES

After three years at The Cove, my dad felt led to move back to Columbia to begin a ministry off his back porch. My parents returned to their home there, and from that time on my father never made a salary. He put his own money into his ministry and lived off his investments for the next twenty-five years.

I would call this working for the Master and giving 100 percent. I think Dad would call it making up for lost time. It was as if he was trying to make up for the years that he had run his own life and given to God's work only when he felt like it. "It's not for our prosperity, but for our posterity that we are making these changes," my parents would say. My father and mother had seen so many ministry leaders abuse the money they raised that they never took one dime in salary from their ministry. They only put money into it. It was just something they felt led to do.

They called their new ministry Laity Alive and Serving, and it was dedicated to helping all the Harry Dents out there who were sitting in pews and spending their lives going to church without really knowing what God's big picture is all about. And it was dedicated to all the Betty Dents in the church who had good intentions but don't know the Bible well enough to make use of its unending resources. The motto of their ministry came from a plaque I had laid under my dad's pillow (where I used to leave things I hoped he would read). It read, "The Purpose of Life is to Serve God."

When my father wrote his second book as a Christian, *Cover Up: The Watergate in All of Us*, he signed my copy with these words: "You were right all along." The following excerpt is from his book:

> Ginny gave me a number of books and tracts. Usually she just left them around, like under my pillow. One day she gave me a plaque. It read: "The Purpose of Life is to Serve God." Today this constitutes the logo of the ministry Betty and I have, "Laity Alive and Serving."
>
> I had told Ginny and Alton they could never be successful—never be accepted into a graduate school. Today Ginny holds two master's degrees and Alton now holds a doctorate in education from the University of South Carolina. He has given his life to Christian lay ministry as a father, educator and church member. He has never attended seminary, but he has sent several people to seminary including his "successful, know-it-all father-in-law."
>
> The Brants have dedicated their lives to helping the deaf and hard-of-hearing. Their specialty is education for deaf children. The Brants lead with their lives. They don't preach; they put forward their best sermon, which is what Jesus called salt and light (Matthew 5:13, 14).[1]

My dad was like the Energizer Bunny. Nothing could stop his miraculous search for God's purpose in his life. His baptism of fire was like someone diving off the high dive when they had never gone underwater in a pool before. He was out to make a big splash and to save all the old Harry Dents in the pew. Nothing could stop him.

Dad might have been out of politics and law as full-time professions, but he certainly kept busy. As he was building Laity Alive and Serving, he also threw himself into serving with his Southern Baptist denomination. He began speaking in churches throughout the denomination, sharing his testimony, exhorting the church to live wholeheartedly for Christ and teaching God's big picture from Genesis to Revelation. He traveled increasingly. My parents were members of First Baptist Church in Columbia, and Dad had a special affinity for the choir, which was directed by Steve Phillips; he loved to hear the orchestra and the choir perform. But because of his many speaking engagements, he was rarely able to be at his home church.

Although he considered himself a Christian above all, Dad's service to his denomination as a Southern Baptist occupied a great deal of his time. As his involvement grew in the late 1980s and through the '90s, he faithfully served as a trustee of Southern Seminary in Louisville, Kentucky, and as a trustee of Charleston Southern University in Charleston, South Carolina. He also served as a member of the Executive Committee of the Southern Baptist Convention.

A Christian Author in the Making

My father had always been a great speechwriter. He had also been a news correspondent in his early years in Washington. Even so, he had missed the most important information contained in any book, and that was God's plan of salvation from Scripture. Once my father saw the big picture of what the Bible was all about and understood God's plan for humankind, he wanted to make sure others didn't miss what he had for so many years.

So as he shared these truths verbally in his travels for Laity Alive and Serving and for the Southern Baptist Convention, he also wrote *A Layman Looks through the Bible for God's Will*, a review of the whole Bible detailed with both text and charts. He was convinced that all Christians needed to understand things from God's point of view as revealed in His Word. The book was first printed in 1983 and was reprinted six times. It is a valuable tool for any pastor or layperson in understanding the purpose of each book in the Bible and the redemptive plan of God.

In 1984 Dad felt led to write about his Watergate experiences. *Cover Up: The Watergate in All of Us* was first published in 1985. He told specifically how Watergate affected his own life, as well as those of many of the men and families he worked with. To my father, the lessons of Watergate took us back to the Garden of Eden, where the first humans failed to admit the wrong they had done and instead tried to cover it up. In 1986 a special edition of the book was given to members of Congress, the White House and the Supreme Court and to other key leaders in Washington and South Carolina.

In 1992 my parents published a book together called *Right Versus Wrong: Solutions to the American Nightmare.* In this book they reveal how they survived their own upbringings in broken and alcoholic homes as well as their own mistakes in parenting. They wrote that although they had had good intentions from the beginning, they had come to realize that intending to do the right thing wasn't enough. And even when they had done the right thing, they had discovered that their good works couldn't save them. Finally, they realized that as a couple they must connect to God as their source in order to carry out His plan in their lives. Mom and Dad revealed how they moved from being part of the problem in America to being part of the solution.

Overseas Ministry

In 1986 my parents traveled to Amsterdam with the Billy Graham Crusade. This was the beginning of their overseas ministry, which was to become such a big part of my dad's work afterward. On the last day of the crusade, all crusade attendees were sent out to witness on the streets of Amsterdam. It was a thrill for my mom and dad to be part of that opportunity. Their hearts, however, were broken when they saw many beautiful churches that had been turned into museums, schools, offices and nightclubs.

Harry and Betty Dent were welcomed with open arms when they went to South Korea in October of 1987 on a partnership evangelism project of the Southern Baptist Convention. They helped the Korean Baptist Convention with house-to-house wit-nessing and church revival services. My father had been an army lieutenant who had once served in the Korean War; now his purpose was to save the South Koreans from Communism and to stop the party's worldwide spread. He was impressed with the South Koreans' spiritual fervor, childlike faith and sense of com-mitment. My parents had an awesome experience being part of praying in unison with the South Koreans. (They all prayed their own prayers at the same time. The noise level was unbelievable and inspiring to hear.)

My father also noted that there had been a substantial in-dustrial recovery in South Korea, which had been helped in part by the United States of America. The spiritual miracle in South Korea had also been influenced by America, through its mission-aries and American military personnel and their families.

My parents clearly saw from their trip that the Lord was using South Korea as a beacon in the East. The population of Christians in this country had grown explosively, especially dur-ing the 1980s. Some of the people there felt that the catalyst for their spiritual revolution was, as in other places, the Billy Graham Crusade, which had been held in South Korea in 1971.

From South Korea my parents traveled to China, where they saw a covert spiritual revolution. They saw many house churches and estimated that there were several million "hidden Chris-tians" in China, in contrast to what they had seen in South Ko-rea, where Christianity was out in the open.

Almost twenty years later I traveled to China and attended underground churches, ministering to three thousand people in one week. In just twenty years, from the time my parents had first visited China, the number of believers went from several million to an estimated 80 to 150 million, which is 5 to 10 percent of the national population—and this in a country where worshiping Jesus Christ is against the law. The tremendous growth of the church in China clearly shows us that no govern-ment can stifle God's message and power. My parents and I saw firsthand that political freedom is not necessary in order for God to work in people's hearts.

My dad went to Australia in 1987 with Leighton Ford, Billy Graham's brother-in-law, where the churches asked him to return to teach the Bible using the overhead transparencies he had created for giving his lessons on Genesis through Revelation. He returned in 1989 for six weeks, taking my mother with him. They spoke in fifteen schools, a university, a youth camp, a rotary club and on several television and radio stations. My dad taught his Bible survey course, which gives the "big picture of the Bible" from Genesis to Revelation, in seventeen churches.

There were fewer churches per capita in Australia than in Europe, and they were smaller and had minimal budgets (due to not having tax-exempt status). But the believers were very committed. They stayed in the meetings as long as Dad would teach—and because my dad can be long-winded and sometimes forget that it is time to stop, that's saying a lot.

In 1991 my parents made a trip to Russia and Romania, and on the way back stopped in England. There they found that people would discard any free literature given to them and that many of the churches were void of worshipers. My mom and dad were burdened when they realized that England, once known as the "Beacon of Light to the World," was dimming its own light.

As my parents traveled in these ministry years, they were thrilled to share the gospel in so many places around the world.

Easter behind Bars—and a New Partnership

Working with my dad in his ministry was one of the greatest joys of my life. It was something I was privileged to do for about fifteen years. We spoke in churches and at retreats together. We were the father-daughter duo, and God's intervention in our lives made for a powerful story. Our working together started in 1988, when my husband was out of town one weekend. I received a last-minute request from my dad: "Ginny, Chuck Colson is coming to town to do an Easter service at the Perry

Correctional Institute in Pelzer. We need someone to add some special music. Can you help us out?"

"I'll see if I can find a babysitter for your grandsons," I replied. "Alton is out of town." By this time Alton and I had been blessed with three boys: Joshua, now six, and twins Jonathan and Harrison, three.

I began thinking about his request. Perry was a maximum-security prison. The last time my father had ministered in that prison, in 1985, a breakout had occurred the day after he preached. An inmate and his wife had replicated a scene from the Charles Bronson movie *Breakout* and escaped in a helicopter. The getaway had made international news.

I began searching for a babysitter, only to find there were none available. I began to wonder what my husband would think if I took our three young sons with me. I called my father back to tell him my predicament, and he said, "Just bring the kids along. Your mother will be there, and she can watch them on the prison playground while we go in for the service."

Reluctantly, I agreed, still concerned about what my husband would say if I could get in touch with him. *Surely*, I thought, *no prisoner will take us hostage to escape.* I began to prepare my music for the service.

I had a lump in my throat as we approached the prison. Before entering the property, we stopped at a McDonald's to get my sons Happy Meals. Again I reassured myself, *Surely they won't have a breakout today.*

My hands twitched as we neared the much-feared facility which housed murderers, rapists and thieves. But Jesus had shown compassion for everyone, and I need to do the same. *Lord, please protect my three sons.*

We all entered through the security gate and then the iron doors. I heard the gates and doors close behind me, and I knew there was no turning back. I kissed my sweet sons' precious cheeks and sent them to the playground to eat their Happy Meals with my mom.

Chuck Colson, my dad and I edged further into the tightly sealed institution. We passed through two more sets of security doors before finally reaching our destination. The rooms were dark, cool and uninviting. It was Easter. Jesus had risen. And we were to celebrate the Good News behind bars with men who faced persecution from other inmates just for attending our event.

I sang "The Day He Wore My Crown" in voice and in sign language. I made sure each man who came received the message of the song audibly and visually. I was amazed at their attention and the tears in their eyes as I sang. When I finished, you could have heard a pin drop.

My father stepped up to give his testimony. "I came close to standing in your shoes. But God delivered me from myself at age forty-eight. My life has never been the same. Today I am free in Christ. Those of you who are bold enough to do as I did can be freed from yourselves, too." The prisoners immediately identified with my father and his heart for their situation. They labored on every word that came from his mouth.

Then Chuck Colson preached about the kingdom of God and about freedom in Christ. Again, tears flowed from many eyes. It was the most moving Easter service I had ever attended. I got chills up and down my spine. There, behind bars, men who had given their lives to Christ were able to experience true freedom in Him.

I stayed after the service to shake hands with these dear brothers in Christ who had boldly displayed their allegiance that day. Some were about to be released, some had more time to pay, and some would never be able to leave. But many of their faces told the story of changed lives. Though they were behind three sets of prison doors and locks, nothing could separate them from the love of Christ. And only in Him can we find true freedom.

Bob McAlister, my dad's friend from Thurmond days who eventually served as chief of staff to South Carolina Governor Carroll Campbell, painted another picture of my father. Bob,

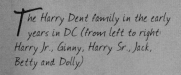

*T*he Harry Dent family in the early years in DC (from left to right: Harry Jr., Ginny, Harry Sr., Jack, Betty and Dolly)

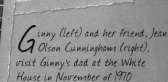

*G*inny (left) and her friend, Jean Olson Cunningham (right), visit Ginny's dad at the White House in November of 1970

*D*olly Dent Montgomery (far left) and Ginny (far right) with Julie Nixon Eisenhower at the White House, planning Mamie Eisenhower's seventy-fifth birthday celebration

*G*inny and her high-school sweetheart (later husband) Alton Brant in 1971

*G*inny Dent Brant wins Miss Senior at the Miss Spring Valley High School pageant in 1973

*M*odeling shots from Ginny's portfolio.

*F*rom the Associated Press, August 17, 1969
"Nixon's inner circle has set up a smooth machine"

*H*arry Dent meets with President Nixon in the Oval Office in February 1973

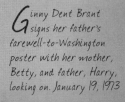

*G*inny Dent Brant signs her father's farewell-to-Washington poster with her mother, Betty, and father, Harry, looking on. January 19, 1973

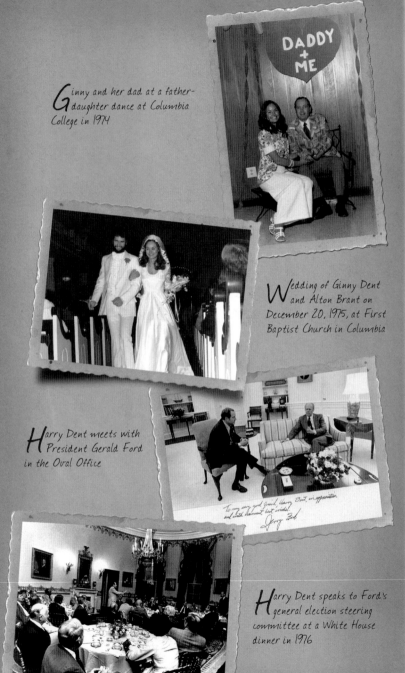

*G*inny and her dad at a father-daughter dance at Columbia College in 1974

*W*edding of Ginny Dent and Alton Brant on December 20, 1975, at First Baptist Church in Columbia

*H*arry Dent meets with President Gerald Ford in the Oval Office

*H*arry Dent speaks to Ford's general election steering committee at a White House dinner in 1976

*H*arry Dent with President
Ronald Reagan

*G*inny, son Joshua and Alton
Brant with Senator and Nancy
Thurmond at the Senate Dining Room
in 1983

Best wishes to my good friend
Alton Brant and his beautiful
and talented wife Ginny Dent
Brant. Strom Thurmond
U.S.Senator - S.C.

*H*arry and Betty Dent
with President and
Mrs. George H. W. Bush at
the White House

To Betty and Harry Dent
with best wishes,
G. Bush   Barbara Bush

*H*arry Dent with his prized
gift from a Romanian
nurse who had climbed to seize
it—the Romanian flag with the
Communist symbol cut out

*G*inny and Harry in Timișoara, Romania, on the square where the Revolution started.

*H*arry Dent preaching with a bullhorn with a Romanian interpreter in Cluj, Romania, in 1991

*R*omanics from South Carolina with Josef Tson, former president of the Romanian Missionary Society, in 1991: Tom and Arlene Beal, Greg and Bobbie Horton, Harry and Betty Dent, Josef and Elizabeth Tson, Alastair and Ginny Walker, Benny and Magaly Littlejohn

*H*arry speaks to the Romanian Senate

Harry and President Ion Iliescu of Romania

Harry and Betty Dent with Billy Graham at the South Carolina Billy Graham Crusade in 1987

Kathy Gariety, Bill Koehn and Martha Myers, who paid the ultimate price while serving Christ in Yemen

Martha Myers caring for the people she loved at the hospital in Jibla, Yemen

Jean-ne and Harry Dent Jr.

Clay, Don, Blake, Anna, Dolly and Graham Montgomery

Josh, Sydney, Alton, Ginny, Jonnie and Harrison Brant

Harry, Sarah, Lizy, Jack and Tracie Dent

Betty and Harry Dent

who now runs a public relations firm and a death row ministry in Columbia, watched Dad one time as he taught a Bible study to death row and prison inmates on a dirty concrete floor in one-hundred-degree temperatures. "These inmates," said Bob, "who had been shunned by their own families, could not believe that a man like Harry Dent would care about them. But he did." According to Bob, "It was not in the halls of the West Wing, but in the lowly places such as the floors of prisons and the slums of Romania where Harry Dent found fulfillment, and where he discovered real power."[2]

After the Easter service, as Chuck Colson and my dad went to death row to pray with some of the inmates, I went to find my boys. They were playing on the slides and merry-go-rounds and appeared unaware of the barbwire fences all around them. "Look mom, we got a prize in our Happy Meals," Jonathan said. They clutched their toys proudly and walked toward the prison gates. "Mom, where have you been?"

"I've been sharing Easter with some Christian brothers," I replied. Their little minds were too young and innocent to understand where they had been or what had happened that day.

As the last set of locks closed behind us, a tear streamed from my eye. I couldn't help but remember how close my father had come to losing his freedom. My heart was filled with gratitude that he had not. For the men who received Christ that day, losing their earthly freedom had helped them to find true freedom. Now they were living for eternity, or as my pastor Ken Lewis would say, they were living for the line (eternity), not for the dot (the here and now).

"We had a fun time, Mom, thanks for taking us," Josh spoke up. My boys had their toys to remember the event. I just hoped their daddy would express the same sentiment they did.

We arrived home about the same time as my husband. "Where have you been with Harry Dent's most prized possessions?" he asked.

"You would never believe me if I told you," I replied. I was nervous that he might be upset that I had put our boys in danger.

When he first heard my story, he was a little surprised. "You really took my boys to that place? You're not kidding me, are you?" But when I told him what had happened that day, he understood, patting me on the hand.

That Easter took on new meaning for me. Freedom from bondage to sin is a precious gift indeed. You can have it behind bars.

14

SOCIAL CONCERNS FOR THE SAKE OF CHRIST

Besides sharing Christ with men in prison, my father and Chuck Colson both ministered to people they had formerly worked with in the political world. My father wanted to give to others what he himself had gained. Lee Atwater, a former consultant and strategist for the Republican Party known for his aggressive and often ruthless tactics, was one such individual. As soon as Lee learned he had an inoperable malignant brain tumor, he tracked my father down to share his devastating news with him. "Harry," he said, "I don't have much time left on this earth, and I need you to fly up here and tell me everything you know about God."

Dad didn't hesitate and got on a plane as soon as he could. He remembered when he had felt led to tell Atwater, several years back, "We need a kinder and gentler Lee." My father spent ten hours with him that day, praying, reading the Bible and explaining what God's big picture was all about. Lee had consulted with many people of different religions before this. He was a man who was searching, and he had a lot to ponder in a short period of time.

At my father's request, Chuck Colson paid his own timely visit to Lee. Doug Coe of the Fellowship Foundation also spent many hours with him when he was at the end of his rope.

The compelling evidence of Christianity moved Lee to end his search, and he surrendered his life to Jesus Christ.

Lee Atwater was the man who had once gotten his kicks from pulling the rug out from under his political opponents. Now he was following the Golden Rule. He wanted the world to know that he had found Jesus Christ while he still had time to share with people. The things he had once counted as all-important in life, things like power, fame and glory, no longer had meaning to him. Repentance, love, family and relationships became the most important things.

He showed that he had genuinely begun a new chapter in life when he sought forgiveness from those he had hurt during his political career. One of the people he apologized to was my father. When Bush, Reagan and Connally were seeking the Republican nomination in 1980, Lee had planted a story about John Connally and attributed the negative propaganda to my dad. This mean-spirited act had followed my father throughout his life.

According to Dad's friend Bob McAlister, Atwater confronted life's key question: What does it profit a man if he gains the whole world and loses his own soul? Sadly, Lee died several months after coming to Christ. It was my father who preached the sermon at his funeral service, which was televised from Trinity Episcopal Cathedral in Columbia on March 31, 1991. Lee's greatest fear had been facing death, but he learned how to face it with grace kneeling at the foot of the cross of Calvary.[1]

It's Character that Counts

If you were going to work on Senator Thurmond's staff, you were expected to be a person of integrity and character. The senator delighted in the hiring of such people. Dad always felt that his Boy Scout training had contributed to his own character growth—and had kept him from being involved in the Watergate scandal in the years before he became a Christian. It was his scout leader, Roger Kirk, who became a role model to him after my dad's grandfather died.

My father believed a person's basic character is formed early in life. His own character had essentially been formed through the scouting program. In today's society there seems to be a lack of character education in the formative years of our children. Through my eyes as a public school teacher and counselor, I too could see the moral decline in America. It grieved my father and I both to see what was happening to children.

My father was committed to the virtues of honesty, justice, compassion, integrity, duty, self-control, responsibility and respect. And he felt that the home was the first place such things should be taught. My father saw the breakdown of the family as the main problem in America. The church was another place that character should be taught, but the breakdown of the family was directly associated with a decline in church attendance. That left the schools.

In 1995 my father began a one-man crusade to introduce character training in the schools of South Carolina. He worked with Dr. Ben Nesbitt, assistant deputy director at the State Department of Education, and with Dr. Barbara Nielson, superintendent of schools in South Carolina. He wrote the book *Teaching Jack and Jill Right Versus Wrong* in 1996 to be used as a primer in the schools.

My father was well aware that we were not able to have religious teaching in the public schools, but he felt we could use the great universal moral virtues to teach our children right versus wrong. He saw nothing wrong with teaching public school students these things. He was willing to do whatever he could for the sake of his children and grandchildren. My dad knew that it was best when the home, school and church worked in harmony to teach and model character, as a child would be more likely to apply it in his or her life. But having at least one place where children could receive education in these values was better than none.

For his work with character education in South Carolina,

Dad was known as the "father of character education in South Carolina" and was given the Golden Apple Award by the South Carolina Department of Education.

Standing for Convictions

One man my father supported politically, believing he would bring his convictions to his elected position, was David Beasley. Dad and a group of couples prayed for and supported Beasley's run for governor of South Carolina in 1994, which he won.

During his term, Beasley became known as a man who brought his Christian faith into the public arena. He tried to outlaw video poker machines in the state because he felt it was ruining families. He also started a program called Putting Families First in which churches and groups would adopt a family on welfare and assist them to become independent of government aid. My sister, Dolly Montgomery, and her family participated in this program. They adopted a single African American woman with three children. Eventually the woman was able to support herself and end her dependence on the government.

But what David Beasley became most known for was his compromise position on moving the Confederate flag from the top of the state capitol to a Confederate memorial on the capitol grounds. My father was his friend, and told him, "David, you *do* have to do the right thing; you *don't* have to be governor next term." After a series of racial incidents in the state, including arson at some black churches, the governor felt the flag had to come down.

Beasley continued in his convictions, and my dad's words to him turned out to be prophetic. He was defeated in his race for reelection. Even so, my father and I felt he had done the right thing. In 2003 Beasley was awarded the John F. Kennedy Profile in Courage Award by Caroline Kennedy and US Senator Ted Kennedy for his controversial decision to remove the Confederate flag from the South Carolina capitol. I think history will remember him as a hero.

While serving as governor, David Beasley lost his chief legal counsel, Henry Deneen, when Henry left politics to attend seminary. Eventually, Henry and his wife Celia would end up on the mission field. The close tie between the Beasleys and the Deneens continues today. In April of 2005 Beasley and Deneen started the Center for Global Strategies, a ministry focusing on bringing business, healthcare, government and educational resources to the emerging world. During his term, Beasley had told my father he would like to be involved in missions one day. He felt God calling him to a greater purpose after his work as governor of South Carolina. And so another politician eventually stepped out of his comfort zone to join God in His work in our world.

When my father left the field of politics in 1981, he knew God was calling him for a special purpose. Even though there were many attractive offers to serve the people, my father wasn't about to abandon God's call for any amount of money, security or fame. He had already missed out on forty-eight years of serving God by following his own agenda. For the remaining years of his life, he would follow God's agenda, with my dear mother right by his side. And God's plan was still unfolding with yet more to come.

15

TEAMING UP WITH THE PERSECUTED BRETHREN IN ROMANIA

In July of 1990, my father felt led to go with Rev. John Guest on a short ministry trip to Romania. This was approximately six months after the fall of Communism there. My father was keenly aware of what had happened in that country and felt for the people who had endured such repression for so many years. Dr. Guest was setting up crusades in several major Romanian cities; my father would go to help with the crusades, speak in churches and teach pastors and laypeople through the Romanian Missionary Society. Dad ended up in a beautiful city called Cluj in the heart of Transylvania, surrounded by hills and mountains.

Romania had entered World War I on the side of the Allies in 1916. Ironically, at the beginning of World War II, the country of Romania aligned with Hitler, because they saw him as the lesser of two evils—Communism being the other. The one thing the students and intellectuals of Romania didn't want was Communism, so they stood against the Soviet Union. It was in 1944 that they realigned themselves with the Allies.

Romania had always been rich in agriculture, minerals and oil. In an effort to stop Hitler's utilization of Romania's rich oil supply to fuel his Nazi machine, the United States destroyed much of the country's highly prized oil fields. Then, when the war was over, the Russians invaded. The land was plundered, polluted and impoverished under Communism, for the benefit of the elite, for forty years. Romania suffered at the hands of Germany, the Soviet Union and, although without deliberate intention, the United States.

After World War II, Romania became one of the Communist Bloc's most oppressive and cruel regimes. The greedy and megalomaniacal rule of Nicolae Ceauşescu brought the entire country of Romania to ruins. Human rights abuse was the rule of his administration.

Ironically, in 1966, Ceauşescu was featured on the cover of *Time* magazine. The article inside, entitled "Eastern Europe—Life under a Relaxed Communism," declared that the Romanian president was seeking to meet his country's needs and build a better Romania for the people. Ceauşescu ended up visiting the White House several times and received prestigious honors on each of his visits. President Nixon thought highly of him and saw Ceauşescu as someone who could contribute to the resolution of the world's most urgent global problems. The Romanian leader also visited Great Britain in 1978 and met Margaret Thatcher as well as the Queen of England. None of these leaders seemed to see Ceauşescu for the despot he really was. They had no idea he was talking one way to international leaders but acting to the contrary within his own country. Ceauşescu was a diabolical deceiver.

Mikhail Gorbachev, however, was visibly upset when he came to Romania in 1987 and saw the condition of the country. Ceauşescu always managed to appease Gorbachev by telling him that all was well in Romania, but nothing could have been further from the truth. While he claimed that his people had plenty to eat, in actuality they had only scraps on their tables. Gorbachev embarrassed Ceauşescu before his own people on this visit when he gave a speech in Bucharest, saying that "half a truth is worse than a lie."

Ceauşescu's regime was finally toppled in December of 1989. On December 15 the church stood their ground in protest against the Communist government as it sought to displace pastor László Tőkés from his home in Timişoara. Within five days the crowd of protestors had grown to approximately 100,000 people at the Piaţa Victoriei (formerly known as Opera Square but today called Victory Square, it is the symbol of the Romanian Revolution). The people refused to back down, even when the Communist army shot them down in the streets. It was estimated that more than one thousand protesters died throughout Romania during those days of revolution, including some, I am told by friends, in the city of Cluj. In a country in which the secret police and the media controlled the government, no one knows for sure the precise number of people who perished. A military tribunal executed Ceauşescu and his wife on Christmas Day after a brief trial.

Before the revolution, in 1985, Ceauşescu had allowed Billy Graham to preach in several churches, including the Romanian Orthodox Churches in Timişoara and in Cluj. In Timişoara alone over 150,000 people came to hear Dr. Graham's preaching, although Ceauşescu had limited the audience only to those who could fit inside the cathedral. In looking back, I wonder if Graham's visit had anything to do with the revolution. Several have speculated that the church was starving for the truth and that once they heard it, they wanted more. This may be the reason these Christians stood against Ceauşescu's heinous regime.

Stirrings from other revolts probably impacted the Romanian Revolution as well. In 1956 there was an uprising in Hungary. Intellectuals and highly educated people staged a rebellion in Czechoslovakia in 1968. Pope John Paul II inspired a revolt in Poland in his earlier years, when he was living under Communism. In 1987 another outbreak started in a tractor factory in Braşov, Romania. The Communist armies squelched each of these attempts, and participants were either killed or severely punished. All of these were ripples that produced a greater wave to come.

Dr. Josef Tson was a Romanian pastor who had been beaten during Romania's Communist years and finally exiled to the

USA. In the States he became president of the Romanian Missionary Society, founded in 1968 by Dr. Peter Trutza; the RMS was an organization dedicated to serving Romanian Christian trapped behind the Iron Curtain. Tson said, "The Communists *promised* heaven on earth, but they *produced* hell on earth. Communism looks great—but it tastes horrible." Under Communism, if believers refused to join the party, their careers were negatively affected. Those with a "born-again" attitude paid a high price for their faith, including being beaten, imprisoned and executed. Tson contends that we in the West are falling for the delusion of Communism and slowly moving toward it.

Even after Communism's fall in Romania, economic recovery has been slow in the country, hindered by the stain that the party left on the government through its resistance to change and its bloated bureaucracy. The revolution and succeeding elections have failed to separate this country from its Communist past. Even today many of the elected officials are former Communists.

According to Ian Fisher of the *New York Times*, Romania had the toughest transition out of Communism than any other former Soviet state. He believes that the cruel dictatorship of Ceauşescu, the fact that the old Communist guard took over after he was executed, and the profound poverty and fear of change among many ordinary Romanians are primary reasons for this. Romanian economic reform has lagged far behind most of Central Europe in developing a market economy.[1]

Harry Dent Arrives in Cluj

It was into this situation my father came shortly after the dramatic revolution and fall of Romanian Communism. The fields were ripe unto harvest: the John Guest Crusades were credited with over seven thousand converts. My father was impressed with how many opportunities there were to bring people to the Lord.

He had never imagined that he would one day preach on the street with a bullhorn, but in Romania he did. He learned to preach this way, using an interpreter and a brass band or singer, in the downtown streets of Cluj and in the villages. And it was the greatest experience of his life. He was actually overrun by people moving forward to receive Christ and to grab a piece of Christian literature. In some ways it was like the stumping he had done in his earliest days in politics—only now he did it with a life-changing spiritual message.

My father called home many times to tell us about Romania and what was happening in that country. In his excitement, though, he failed to notice the hour at which he was calling.

"I did it, I really preached with a bullhorn," he excitedly reported. "You can't imagine the number of people who wanted to hear more. God has created a spiritual hunger in these people I've never seen before."

"I only wish we were there with you to see it," I responded.

"You've just got to come and experience the work of God here. Alton would love it," he said. "I've never seen anything like it. You know what would happen to me if I did this same thing in the USA."

"Yes, I know. You'd be laughed off the streets, possibly arrested for not having a permit. One day, Dad, I promise I'll go with you," I said with a tear in my eye. It may have been 2:00 a.m., but the thrill in his voice was a welcome sound. Here was God's promise to me, made long ago on that tear-filled day when I was driving to CIU, being much more than fulfilled before my very eyes. God had told me then that He would take care of what was troubling me—namely, my dad's opposition to my attending CIU. The man who had forbidden me to attend Columbia International University was now living out the school's motto, "To Know Him and Make Him Known."

It was a sad reality that Dad wouldn't have had the same response in the land of the free and the home of the brave. In Romania the doctrine of Communism had created a spiritual hunger, and the underground church was struggling to come to the surface. My dad marveled that God actually had a plan to use Communism for His own purposes. Through his work with the John Guest crusade, my dad immediately identified with the persecuted Christian brethren who had faced oppression, suffering and restriction in everything they did. Despite what they had endured, the Romanians were the most gracious people my dad ever encountered. He could not talk about the brethren in Romania without tears pooling in his eyes.

God Had a Plan All Along

Harry Dent was a man who, early in his college years, had felt a calling to politics to help save the world from Communism. I have heard both my parents say that this was the primary reason my father stepped into the political arena. It was more than a career path—it was an ideology he embraced, which first led him into service in the Korean War and later to his work in Washington. But now, as a Christian, God would use him to empower and assist Romania in her recovery from Communism. When my father attended the White House dinner in 1970 which recognized and celebrated the accomplishments of Ceauşescu, little did he know that he would one day help Romania recover from the effects of that dictator. I now see that it was all part of God's larger plan.

As a result of the John Guest Crusade in 1990, my father was invited to meet with the mayor of the city of Cluj and the governor of the county of Cluj. My father told them both directly, "We are happy Communism is over, and we are here to help you."

The governor replied, "We did not ask for Communism. It was imposed upon us by the Red Army. Your country's president, Stalin and Churchill handed us over to Communism on a paper napkin."

Kneeling on the floor of the main hall of a government building, my father said, "I am very sorry for this mistake made by my country. But I am here, and I promise to help your people as long as I shall live."

My father repeated this apology several times in his travels around the impoverished country. I am told by many Romanians, whom my family would grow to trust, that this apology helped the healing process for them and for others who heard of it. When my father would go into the villages, the elderly people would say, "After World War II, we waited for the United States to rescue us, but you never came." But now these elderly people were relieved to see Americans there to help. All of this burdened my father's heart, and he wanted to help make right what Roosevelt, Stalin and Churchill had done to the good people of Romania.

My father began by putting together a sister-city relationship between Cluj and Columbia, South Carolina. It meant that Columbia would help support Cluj financially and with medical, business and political training. The mayor of Cluj did not want to come to the John Guest crusade, because he was wary of any religion, but my father convinced him it would be a good idea and would help build the sister-city relationship. After attending the crusade, the mayor said, "John Guest is for real, and I would like to be invited back to hear him again. The kind of religion he preached to us tonight is what my people need in their hearts."

The Romanian people needed everything from spiritual renewal to economic growth, from social and humanitarian reform to the rebuilding of the country's infrastructure. As my father promised the mayor of Cluj, he worked hard to ensure the establishment of the sister-city relationship between Cluj and Columbia. (And whenever my father gave his word that he would help, you could count on it.) It was a relationship that would help Romanian people socially, medically, economically, politically and educationally.

With the help and cooperation of Columbia's Mayor Bob Coble, the Columbia Chamber of Commerce, members of the World Affairs Council including Congressman Joe Wilson, and the doctors at Providence Hospital and the USC Medical

School, this relationship was formed and became a blessing to the city of Cluj.

Through this partnership, Columbia's Providence Hospital and the University of South Carolina Medical School joined with the Heart Institute in Cluj and applied to the US State Department for a shared grant of $2 million. My father helped mediate this process. The ensuing financial gift was able to provide for training to the Cluj doctors in open heart and valve replacement surgery. The grant also provided for medical equipment and supplies. Doctors from Providence Hospital also traveled to Cluj to train doctors there. Part of the agreement with the Cluj hospital was that in exchange for the equipment and training, the hospital would have to agree to help those individuals who couldn't afford healthcare. When my father presented the name of a Romanian Christian brother who needed heart surgery but had no means to pay, the heart institute of Cluj took care of his medical needs.

All this assistance offered to the Romanian people was a great testimony for the Christians. The old Communist bosses in that country were now coming to the Americans, the friends of the persecuted brethren, for help in reviving a basically destroyed infrastructure.

After that first visit in 1990, my father returned to Cluj several times each year for almost ten years, bringing other South Carolinians with him. During the 1990s, helping the good people of Romania became my father's overseas passion. It consumed most of his time and wealth, and he did it proudly. Those who got involved with him came to be known in our circles as "Romaniacs."

One of my dad's closest Romanian friends was a young man he had met on his first visit. Eugen Stancel was a Romanian engineer and scholar who served on many occasions as my father's interpreter. Eugen was my dad's right-hand man whenever he traveled in Romania, and Dad coordinated all his work through Eugen. Eugen and his wife, Vali, have served alongside my father's ministry without any compensation for nearly eighteen years now. They have become like part of our family, even though an ocean away.

My father's heart was clearly burdened for the persecuted church in Romania, which was struggling, after the fall of Communism, to come to the surface after many years of oppression and persecution. It didn't take my dad long to see that Romanians who had suffered for their faith needed many things in order for the church to become established and to flourish under this new freedom. According to Pastor Frederic Buhler, a pastor in France after World War II and a mentor of our friend Eugen, aggressive action must be taken in the first twenty years after a revolution and after the granting of religious freedom in order for religion to be established among the people. The Romanian church needed materials, training, facilities and simply more pastors.

My dad started by helping with materials, bringing Bibles and other Christian literature from America. The Romanian Missionary Society wanted to use my father's book *A Layman Looks through the Bible for God's Will.* They felt that the simple presentation of the Bible, with the use of charts, was exactly what the pastors and laypeople needed. The book was translated into Romanian, and Laity Alive and Serving paid for the printing. My father also had his book *Cover Up: The Watergate in All of Us*, along with all his teaching transparencies, translated for the Romanian pastors and laypeople. A retired artist friend, Milton Powell, added color pictures to my dad's transparencies. Laity provided overhead projectors so that the Romanian pastors could use these valuable teaching materials. Each pastor was trying to shepherd as many as ten congregations, so teaching materials to aid them were priorities.

My father brought many South Carolinians with him to help carry materials to Romania. He was never sure, however, who benefited the most—the brethren in Romania or the Americans who came to assist. Being in fellowship with their brothers and sisters who had suffered so much for Christ always had an amazing effect on every American who came to help. Many "Romaniacs" left this little country, having given of their lives in many ways, as better people.

16

A CHALLENGING JOURNEY

In June of 1990, while my father was beginning his ministry in Romania, I was elected to serve as a trustee of the International Mission Board (IMB) of the Southern Baptist Convention. As I traveled to Richmond, Virginia, for my first meeting, I had clear ideas about which countries I was willing to visit. Since I was a mother of three children under seven, my choices were limited to countries that I deemed safe.

For several of my years on the board, I was privileged to serve on the Europe/Middle East Committee—my first choice, since my dad's ministry was in Romania. But when the committee split in two—Europe and the Middle East—the IMB's board chairman, Dr. Leon Hyatt, decided I should serve on the Middle East committee.

I was disappointed, and I wrote to Dr. Hyatt, asking if he would consider moving me back to the Europe committee. Trustees were encouraged to go and work alongside the missionaries in their appointed countries, and I wondered if he had considered the danger for me in the Middle East. But Dr. Hyatt kindly declined my request. Despite my disappointment, I was committed to serving wholeheartedly wherever I was placed. Realizing that God sometimes redirects us by closing doors, I discovered that in closing the way to Europe, God was showing me another place where He wanted me to work.

As I opened my heart to this possibility, I began to see that the missionaries in the Middle East needed the trustees to listen and support them more than most missionaries did. I started to listen to the hearts of those who were home on furlough—but I still wasn't interested in visiting the Middle East. Yet God had a plan, and He was setting it in motion.

In 1997 the IMB was questioning whether or not we should continue with our work at a hospital in Yemen. Eastern Europe had opened up to us overnight, and we couldn't fund everything. So it was decided that I would visit the area to evaluate the situation.

For days I had doubts. While I had taken my position on the board as an oath to serve, I was struggling with the unknown dangers of such a trip. I wanted to be on the mission board, but I didn't want to go to that particular field. The hypocrisy of it all unnerved me. If I stayed in my comfort zone, I would be no better than a fraud. I shared my dilemma with Alton, and we prayed about it. In the end, we decided I should go.

The plan was for me to spend several weeks at the IMB hospital in Yemen, gathering information about whether or not to close the hospital, and then report back to the board. The missionaries had begged the trustees on our committee to experience firsthand how God was working in their desert land before we made a final decision.

Shortly after I made my decision to go, one of our doctors was kidnapped in Yemen and later miraculously escaped. I began to have doubts again, but I knew the area director would let me know if it was too dangerous to go. I decided not to read the news too much, or I might never get on the plane.

Ironically, while my dad was traveling back and forth to Romania to help in her transition toward freedom, I was traveling to places where freedom was practically nonexistent.

Culture Shock

Despite my fears, I boarded the plane with my colleagues

Dale and Anita Thorne and determinedly headed for the Middle East. We traveled by way of Jordan, where we spent four days visiting our workers there. Jordan was so westernized that I didn't initially feel any great culture shock. I enjoyed those four days, seeing many ways that God was working. Before we left for Yemen, I bought ten Arabic Bibles from a Christian bookstore to share along my journey. I packed them inside brown paper bags underneath my undergarments. Then I grabbed a last Quarter Pounder with cheese at an Arabic McDonald's before boarding the plane.

As the airplane video screen repeatedly showed the direction to Mecca during our flight, my body and spirit sensed that I was entering a dark place. When the call to prayer came at 5:00 a.m., I glanced across the aisle to my right at the man next to me. He was lying prostrate on the floor of the plane. I scanned to the left and saw no one standing. Dale and Anita and I were among the few on the plane who didn't bow.

I was beginning to wonder why I had come on this trip. I had to remind myself that I had made a commitment to the dear servants at the hospital—and I had felt the hand of God directing me to come.

As my plane approached Yemen, a country that is a throwback to the fifteenth century, I could feel the darkness all around me. Yemen, a totally Muslim country, became a republic in 1962 and had been closed to the gospel for more than thirteen hundred years. It is a destitute land, unlike its wealthy oil-rich neighbors.

When the plane landed in Yemen's capital Sana'a in the very early morning hours, the culture shock hit full force. I knew immediately that I was in a land far different from my own. Everyone was dressed in black from head to toe except for the three of us Americans. My nose was consumed with strange, pungent smells.

I was the only traveler whose luggage didn't come up on the conveyer belt. I waited and waited—and sweated and sweated. I could feel the perspiration streaming down my face and back. It felt like it was 115 degrees, and there was no air-conditioning. I looked for a restroom. When I entered what appeared to be the ladies' room, I canvassed the room for a toilet. All I saw were several holes in the floor; I decided to pass.

It took hours for my luggage to finally pop up on the scene, and when it did, there were large white Xs on each bag. The customs agents took me to a secured area and began opening my luggage, searching every nook and cranny. I noticed Dale and Anita on the other side of the security gate, looking up and praying.

Then I remembered the smuggled Bibles I had placed in my luggage. My mind sent my body into shock as I wavered between sweating bullets and wetting my pants. *What will they do if they find my Bibles?* I thought. *And what will I say?* So I began thinking up answers in case the inevitable happened. My half-functioning mind came up with silly comebacks like, *I didn't know those were in there!* Or, *Are those Bibles? I just picked them up for fun in Jordan.* Or, *Oh, I can't even read them—they are Greek, I mean Arabic, to me!* Or better yet, *I love to share—would you like one?* Here was a girl who had known nothing but freedom all her life . . . whose freedoms had suddenly vanished. I suddenly sensed my helplessness, and my total dependence on God.

I watched as they opened every compartment in my suitcase, section by section. My normally low blood pressure was rising, and I could feel the sweat oozing out of every pore. The security officer placed his hands over the section where my undergarments were and . . . he simply stopped and closed my suitcase. I felt the biggest relief one could imagine. Undergarments had turned out to be great articles under which to hide those precious books!

Now there was the large bag of medical supplies to deal with. It took hours of discussion, and the field leader served as my interpreter. Finally, a government official released me with the medical supplies, saying, "After all the Baptists have done for the country of Yemen—take them. No taxes! Welcome to Yemen!" I just breathed a sigh of relief. This city slicker had come to town with a bang.

I have never been so glad to make it to the other side of a security line. The Yemen field leader met us and took us to a guesthouse where we could lay down for a few hours; I had slept very little over the last few days and was desperately in need of rest. I lay on the bed, totally exhausted, and examined the door jamb in front of me. Not one side of it was plumb, so how could I shut the door? Then I noticed that not one wall was properly aligned either. After a short nap I got up, excited about taking a bath until I realized I had only several gallons of cold water. I love nothing more than a long, hot bath or shower, but water was too scarce in Yemen for that luxury. I had to admit, though, that the cool water did feel good, since the temperatures continued to soar upward.

Later that afternoon, the field leader took me to the *souk* (market) so I could see the city. I was disturbed when I saw all the men and boys carrying machine guns on their backs and *jambiyas* (curved daggers) across their chests. This was a crowd I didn't want to get lost in. I stayed very close to the field leader as we wove through the souk. I was getting accustomed to seeing everyone dressed totally in black, with only their eyes showing. And then I remembered the dolls my father had brought me from the Middle East when I was a child. I was finally seeing the place those dolls had come from.

I was slightly tanned, and with my olive complexion and dark eyes, I rather looked like I belonged. But still, I stood out, not because of my face but because of my clothing and my speech. *If I could only put a lock on my mouth and not reveal my southern accent*, I thought. There was no freedom of speech in Yemen, but it didn't matter to me since I was too intimidated to say much anyway. I didn't want to bring attention to myself.

Exploring a souk is a good way to learn about a culture. I couldn't avoid the pungent smell of the meats, frankincense, myrrh and seasonings. It was like a scene out of an Indiana Jones movie. A thoughtful woman offered me a drink of water from a well. *How kind*, I thought, but I had to refuse because bacteria were in the water, and she had offered me the same cup everyone drank from. *I should be the one to offer her water.*

As I plowed through trash and filth piled up to my shins and breathed in the stench of poverty all around me, I looked up to God and asked, Why? *Why were these people born here, and I was born in the best of circumstances amid freedom and luxury?* It humbled me, and at that point, I knew IMB needed to have ministries in countries such as this. These poor souls needed the love of Jesus as much as anyone else. They needed the living water that would never run dry.

That night, while trying to sleep, I found myself squirming in the heat and counting the imperfections in the walls and door jambs as if they were sheep. Even thought I was tired from the day's events, I didn't sleep well.

The next morning we left Sana'a early to travel to the hospital some eight hours away. We began our journey with prayer. We took the same road that our doctor had taken when she was kidnapped. (When her kidnappers had threatened to kill her, she had responded by saying, "I am not afraid to die, because when I die I will go to heaven.")[1] Just the week before my arrival, an American oil executive and his son had been captured here as well. This was a road to be wary of. Not only were we isolated and at risk of extremists, the mountainous road itself was dangerously narrow with hairpin turns and no guardrails.

At the halfway mark, we stopped along the side of the road to take care of necessities. City girl that I was, I couldn't figure out how to accomplish this feat while covered from head to toe with clothing. Instead, I stayed in the car and kept the engine running while everyone else took care of business. Besides, I didn't want a warlord to capture me while I was relieving myself!

After nine hours we made it across the breathtaking mountains. When we arrived, I ran straight to the restroom, about to bust. I became known among my companions as the only person who could go for nine to ten hours without relieving herself—the woman with a bladder of steel!

Our IMB hospital workers had a dinner to welcome me that night. During the meal I was part of a conversation with the field leader and the area director. Their talk unnerved me. They were saying things I did not want to hear, like "We must beware of rabid dogs, as they are traveling in packs around the area." Or "Mosquito nets are a must, because some of our doctors and nurses have contracted malaria and are fighting for their lives." Or "The hospital is on high alert due to threats made against us by a group of men known as al-Qaeda."

"Who are they?" I asked.

"Do you remember the bombing of the World Trade Center in 1993? They're the group responsible for that, and their leader is a man called Osama Bin Laden."

I had never heard that name before. Bin Laden had been born in Yemen, and his family had immigrated to Saudi Arabia and become very wealthy through construction. He was later thrown out of Saudi Arabia and then formed terrorist training camps in Yemen and in other countries.

This was not the polite conversation I was used to. This dialogue had pushed all my buttons; I felt like I had reached my anxiety limit. Just before I went to my room to catch up on the (now) five nights' sleep I had missed, the field leader informed me that the airlines had gone on strike. I was stranded.

Then I remembered how we as a mission board had sent helicopters to rescue missionaries when other countries had become unstable. I informed the field leader that I could call Richmond. After all, one of their trustees was here. I figured if things got dangerous enough, I could have us rescued.

Just when I thought it couldn't get worse, he said, "We don't have air space permission here." In other words, if there was trouble in Yemen, we were stuck. *Great, no freedom of air space here.*

Does anyone have any good news to share? I thought to myself.

I had access to a computer, so I wrote e-mails to my husband and my dad about my possible delay and its reasons. After reading over the e-mail, I decided I would not want to be on the receiving end of that message. So I never sent it. I desperately wanted to talk with my husband and my dad—just to hear their comforting voices. However, I didn't want to alarm them. I was learning to depend on God every moment of every day.

Since we were in a mountainous region, it was finally cool enough for me to sleep. But how could I sleep after hearing about the dogs, the mosquitoes and al-Qaeda? Fear filled my mind, and counting sheep or imperfections in the walls was not going to help. Finally, in the wee hours of the morning, I fell asleep. That night I dreamed that al-Qaeda was all around us and that a helicopter had dropped a ladder from above to rescue me. As I was risking my life to crawl up the ladder to freedom, shouts and chants rang in my ears. Then the unthinkable happened—repeated rounds of machine-gun fire!

To add to my horror, I awoke from my fears hearing real machine guns firing around me. *Are they coming to get this American?* I thought. I thought about the pastors who had recommended me for the IMB, and I was wishing they could change places with me. Soaring from an adrenalin rush from my head to my feet, I ran into the next bedroom and voiced my fears to a young nurse with whom I was staying. "Nothing here appears safe to me," I admitted to her in gasps. "How do you remain so calm?"

I will never forget her response. She very confidently answered me saying, "Safety is being in the middle of God's will." When things became dangerous, or when threats were made (which happened from time to time), the workers would simply pray and then go on working. As I would find in the next few days, that was the mindset of all the workers in Yemen.

The Hearts of Our Workers in Yemen

Dr. Martha Myers was a surgeon and veteran missionary who

had served twenty years at the hospital in the city of Jibla. She dearly loved the people she served, and they dearly loved her. Dr. Myers had been the one who, six months before I arrived in Yemen, had been kidnapped for several days. Miraculously, her life had been spared. That experience would have been enough to send anyone packing for the States, but she continued to serve, never letting fear get in the way.

Early in her life she had felt called by God to go into medical missions. She had been willing to leave the comfort of her sweet Alabama roots to serve in this desolate, restricted wasteland. Her parents, Dr. Ira and Dorothy Myers, raised their children to serve God and encouraged Martha in her adventurous desire to serve so far away. She was known for her home visits to the villages, her long hours at work and her enormous patient load. She was so loving and affectionate; she brought joy to all the village children.

I marveled at how she had sacrificed a big-figure salary as a surgeon in the United States to serve in Yemen. According to her father, Martha refused to fit a pattern—she was unique.[2] While her peers were enjoying the "Have it your way" culture, Martha was learning Arabic.

Bill Koehn, the hospital administrator, was another trouper serving no matter the cost. A head-on collision on a mountain road had left him needing hip replacement surgery. He could have come home and retired early due to his injuries, but instead, he chose to stay and serve the people he loved. I recall so vividly the pain he endured as he and the doctors shuffled me from place to place to show me their work.

On one of our visits, we ended up at a sheik's house. I was properly dressed for this occasion because I was decently covered from head to toe. A nurse had even loaned me a pair of her pants to wear underneath my skirt in case the wind might blow and reveal my ankle. We entered the home and were graciously offered a portion of quat to chew (a narcotic plant that Yemeni chew for hours a day) and the usual narghile water pipe (both of which

I politely declined). Then we sat and talked for hours about the future of the hospital.

The sheik was most grateful for all that the Baptists had done through the hospital. He shared with me that the doctors there had saved his life when he needed heart surgery. After discussing security and the rumors of threats against the hospital, he promised us he would do whatever he could to protect both us and the hospital that had meant so much to his community.

I was finally beginning to relax in this strange environment, and I let down my guard. As we prepared to leave, Bill was in so much pain that he couldn't bend down to tie his shoes. Seeing his trouble, I quickly leaned over to help him. It was what any American would have done. I didn't realize, until all eyes focused on me, that my act of kindness was taboo in this Muslim culture. I had overstepped my boundaries.

In Yemen, women can't look a man in the eye. I was wearing big, dark sunglasses just in case I forgot to behave according to Yemeni culture in this respect. But when I leaned over and tied Bill's shoe, I committed an offensive act. Bill and the doctors quickly relayed my apologies in Arabic to the sheik, and I was spared any punishment. It was a good thing the people of Jibla had a great love for the medical workers. On the journey back to the hospital, the doctors joked about how they had known I was going to mess up. I really put my guard up after that.

Kathy Gariety, the purchasing agent for the hospital, was another fearless worker at Jibla. She fought steadily to keep the hospital running. After visiting the souks and seeing flies all over the meats and vegetables, I had expressed my concern to Kathy as to what would I be eating. *It didn't come from that souk, did it?* She quickly took me into her storage basement and showed me her freezers. All the meats I was to eat had been ordered from France. The workers were so glad a trustee had come for a visit that they rolled out the red carpet. Oh, the relief! I had imagined I might be sitting at a table with all kinds of strange invertebrates and arthropods to eat, but Kathy's gift of hospitality settled my stomach, literally.

Martha, Bill, Kathy and many of their colleagues, knowing that the trustees were debating the question of whether we should keep the hospital open, begged me not to take them from their work assignments. Each of the families in the compound invited me to fellowship with them over a meal. They shared with me how God had led them to this unbelievable place. It was clearly evident to me through hearing each of their personal testimonies that God had indeed led them to their work in Yemen.

I had initially thought that closing the hospital might benefit the workers there whose lives were on the line. But instead, God was showing me He was at work in this place. The freedoms and securities that I often take for granted were not necessary for God to accomplish His work.

To say that my life was touched by the courage, dedication and service of the doctors and nurses at the Jibla hospital would be an understatement. When I was leaving, I told them they were all "Mother Teresas." They demonstrated the love of Jesus to the people of Yemen just as Mother Teresa was then doing to the people of India. Mother Teresa was known for showing rather than telling of her faith, for her encouragement to always "share the love of Jesus, and if necessary, use words." Our hospital workers loved the people of Yemen, and the Yemeni people loved them. It was clear to me that the love of Christ had broken down barriers between the nationals and the hospital workers.

Those servants were "heroes of the faith" to me. They simply viewed their service as following God's will for their lives. They lived in what we might consider primitive and dangerous situations so that the Yemeni people could see Jesus in them. These people were living examples of the character God wants to develop in each of us.

All the workers were there by their own choice. Did they know the dangers? Yes. They had already faced many trials and dangers that we will probably never experience in this country.

But they chose to stay the course. So did I want to take these people away from their calling?

Heavens, no!

It's Okay to Say You're Sorry

The last night I was in Yemen, I learned that simply our consideration of closing down the work there had been hurtful to them. As a representative of the board, I asked them to forgive us. We had never intended to hurt them or to suggest in any way that we didn't appreciate their work. Through our praying together on that last night, there was a sense of healing between the trustees and these dear servants we had unintentionally hurt. We had been rash in our oversight, as we hadn't understood their work from the front lines. It was true that all our budgets were cut and that because of it we would have to do some things differently in Yemen, but I clearly saw that God was at work here.

Before leaving, they again begged me not to take them from their calling. "Don't worry about the danger here. God has called us here, and He will protect us. We also realize that God may be calling us to give our lives to further His work." Those were the words of Bill Koehn—words I would not forget.

When I landed in America, I kissed the good ol' American soil. There had been at least one time in Yemen when I had wondered if I would ever see my father, mother, husband and three sons again. Their sweet faces were a welcome delight. So were air conditioners and modern toilets. But most of all, I had missed my freedoms.

I shared every detail about the trip with my father. My time in Yemen provided me a constant reminder of the freedoms and blessings we so richly enjoy but often take for granted. The testimony of the hospital staff and workers in both countries gave my father, my husband and me a new meaning for the word "freedom."

Within a few weeks I returned to Richmond for another

IMB meeting. After a full report of my trip to the committee, we were all humbled. The members of the Middle East Committee stood solidly behind our dedicated servants and, in the end, did not shut down the hospital. Instead, they expanded the work to include medical clinics all over the country to meet a growing need in Yemen.

I never forgot what our workers told me before I left—that it might be God's will for them to die a martyr's death for the sake of the gospel. For the blood of the martyrs is the seed of the church.

17

THE
REAL
HEROES

My life drastically changed after my trip to the Middle East. My husband was offered a position as a professor in American Sign Language at Clemson University in Clemson, South Carolina, and he accepted. Having lived in Spartanburg for eighteen years, leaving wasn't easy.

We stepped out in faith and moved to Clemson when I too was offered a job in the area, at an elementary school. Our house was on the market, and since we had some people trying to sell their home to buy ours, we took a leap of faith and moved into an apartment in Clemson. Little did we know what was ahead.

We were barely settled when the attacks of September 11, 2001, were carried out—a day none of us will ever forget. My father had predicted years earlier that attacks like this would begin to happen. In the weeks following the tragedy, our potential home buyers decided to stay put. After this, the market for houses like ours literally died.

With one son in college, our twin sons about to enter college, and house and rent payments alongside regular monthly expenses, we were struggling. After 9/11 our safety, freedom, way of life and financial security were threatened. Fear swept through this country like a tidal wave, engulfing every object in its path. And we were the objects—all of us. Then I remembered what the missionaries in Yemen had taught me. They were willing to pay the ultimate price to share the gospel. When I thought about the level of danger they lived under every day, it put everything in perspective.

Weeks turned into months, and then years. It seemed like there was no end to the bills and financial pressures. I was home-sick for Spartanburg and wanted to go back to my old life.

While I was wallowing in my sorrows and feeling the Lord had given me more than I could handle, I was awakened on December 30, 2002, to the startling news that Dr. Martha Myers (the beloved doctor who had been kidnapped), Bill Koehn (the hospital administrator whose shoes I had tried to tie) and Kathy Gariety (the purchasing agent who had ordered my food from France) had been shot and killed by a man influenced by al-Qaeda. Another hospital worker whom I had not met, Donald Caswell, had also been shot, but he was recovering.

The broadcast exploded inside me like the sting of a viper. It's not that I could not believe it; they had warned me five years before that this could happen. No, it was grief that shook me onto my knees. There I was, basking in my own misfortune and selfishness as though my problems were the only ones in the world. And these noble people were standing on the front lines, sacrificing everything.

The Yemeni people who had known Martha, Bill and Kathy mourned after this shooting. They had lost three people they had dearly loved and cherished.

Martha Myers, a Modern-day Lottie Moon

Dr. Martha Myers had been the ever-giving doctor who made house calls. She worked 24/7, answering her beeper no matter what time it rang and often only getting four to five hours of sleep a night. She became so immersed in the Yemeni culture that, although she retained her American Southern cul-ture, she became one of them. Knowing her position there could one day mean her death, she had asked many years before to be buried on the hospital grounds if she should die there. Yemen had become her home after twenty-five years of service.

On her last visit to the States, she told her relatives that it might be her last trip there. It was as though she sensed what lay ahead, and yet she pressed on. Martha had returned home on a rare furlough because her mother was dying of cancer. Her parents were mindful of her calling and encouraged her to return.

During my visit, it was clear to me that Martha intended to stay in Yemen to fulfill her calling, whether we closed the hospital or not. She would live in poverty rather than fail to finish what God had called her to do. She saw beyond the hopelessness, and she, like Mother Teresa, felt Christianity was better communicated by actions than by words. There was no one the Yemeni people loved more than this selfless woman who always gave them a smile.

I couldn't help remembering how I would have characterized Martha when I was sixteen years old and climbing my way to glory in the puffed-up world of modeling. Martha wore no make-up, her clothes were not fashionable, and her face and hands were worn from the sacrifice of caring for others. However, I wasn't sixteen anymore, and God was teaching me slowly but surely what He thought was important in life.

Many women in Yemen would remember the new lease on life Martha had given them when she healed them of leaky bladders, a malady which had formerly left them outcasts. No one would forget her sweet smile, which reflected her true inner beauty. Everyone would remember her kind deeds and her determined message: "Things don't matter . . . people do."[1]

She was never satisfied that she had done enough. She reminded me in a way of Oscar Schindler, who said at the end of World War II, "If only I could have saved one more life."[2] Friends and colleagues described her as a free spirit and a maverick, a modern-day Lottie Moon.[3] When her mother heard the news of her death, she responded with joy, "Martha has beaten me home."[4] The entire Myers family knew this world was not their home.

Bill Koehn, a Father to Many

Bill Koehn was the ever-quiet father figure who had become a shining light for many orphaned Yemeni children. But it was Bill's wife, Marty, who had first felt the call to missions. Bill had worked his way up from bagging groceries to managing a store and was doing quite well for himself when he began to wrestle with God's call on his life to serve.

A nurse at Jibla Hospital described him as a man who was "meek and displayed strength under control."[5] He had shown this control when he had expressed his concern to me about the IMB trustees' proposal to shut the hospital down and to send the workers elsewhere. He had begged me "not to pull the rug out from under all they had labored to do."

It was clear to me that their labor had not been in vain, and their good names were known across the impoverished nation. To me Bill and Martha were the best examples of what Christ spoke about in the Beatitudes in His Sermon on the Mount. Rarely do humans exemplify so well all the character of God. I later learned that Bill meditated on the Sermon on the Mount and strived daily to pattern his life after those beautiful attitudes.[6]

I also remember Bill's childish laugh as he joyfully took me to see the ministry he had developed for Yemeni orphans and the toys he had made for the children.

Despite the head-on collision that had left him disabled, he continued to serve without complaining, although in considerable pain. Bill worked round the clock. He was a man of integrity who knew nothing of life but to give and serve.

After his death, Bill's wife Marty returned to serve in Yemen. Marty told me that as she walked up the steps of her home, half an hour after hearing of her husband's death, God reminded her how Elisabeth Elliot had continued on the mission field of Ecuador after her husband Jim had been killed by Auca Indians in 1956. Elisabeth had eventually gone to live, with her little daughter, among the very people who had speared Jim. It was

God's way of showing Marty what He wanted her to do. As a widow, Marty Koehn grieved with her children and then went back to comfort those who were mourning her husband's death. She served another four years in Yemen before returning to the US.

Kathy Gariety and Her Gifts

Kathy Gariety arrived in Yemen to serve as the hospital's purchasing and supply agent in the summer of 1992. Possessing an independent spirit and a gift of organization, she also brought a much-needed gift of hospitality to the hospital compound. Her first years were a tough adjustment for her, since the country of Yemen had just begun a civil war. But Kathy persevered and was obedient to God's call on her life. Her colleagues described her as the "glue that held the compound together."[7] She could make anyone feel at home, even the doctors and nurses who came from around the world to volunteer. She also operated clothing and food closets for the poor. And in her free time, she kept busy visiting the orphanages.

Kathy's friends and family never quite understood why a single woman would give her life to serve in such a restricted country, where women were treated as second-class citizens. Kathy believed that God did not have boundaries in His heart, and she stayed true to His call through thick and thin. After 9/11 her family urged her to return home for her own safety. Her response to them was clear: "I will continue to stay until God tells me to go home."[8] And God did call her home on December 30, 2002, when she was murdered by a fundamentalist Muslim. She left behind a list of to-dos—and a big hole for someone to fill.

Their Lives Remembered

The International Mission Board of the Southern Baptist Convention held a memorial service in Richmond for the slain workers on January 10, 2003. During the breakfast given before the service, I was able to visit with some of our workers from Yemen who were in the States on furlough. They were grieving, yet hopeful that God would use the tragedy for good. They were actually comforting me.

"Are you afraid to return to Yemen?" I asked them.

"No," they responded, "we're excited about continuing the work."

I also visited with a senior citizen who had served in the Middle East his entire adult life. His two daughters and their families were overseas missionaries as well. One daughter served with her family in Yemen; the other worked with her family in Ethiopia and had been visiting her sister in Yemen when the incident happened.

"Are you concerned about your loved ones?" I asked.

"They are in God's hands, and I trust Him with their care," he responded.

I was truly amazed at his level of confidence. His entire family was in that dangerous place, and yet he felt a sense of peace about it. It was clear he had raised his family to trust and obey God. The fearlessness of these workers and their eagerness to return to a difficult situation simply amazed me.

Then someone's cell phone rang with a call from Yemen. The caller reported that the hospital workers, before the funeral, had been unable to find Dr. Myers' famous beeper that had gone everywhere with her. They were calling to say that they had finally realized they had buried her with her beeper! We all looked at each other and couldn't help but laugh a little. It was appropriate for her beeper to be buried with her—it had become a part of her. God had given us a moment of humor in our time of grieving.

The Response from the Yemeni People

As for the people of Yemen, they lined the streets leading to the hospital to show their grief. They made caskets for God's three beloved servants, and they dug the graves with their own hands. They were angry with the Muslim extremist who had committed the dastardly act. The extremist had feared the Christian influence in his country. He was sentenced to die six months later.

The other hospital workers were grieving yet staying the course. Martha Myers and Bill Koehn's requests to be buried on a hill above the hospital were granted. To this day, their graves serve as reminders of their faithfulness, witness and love for the Yemeni people. What their enemies meant for evil, God has continued to use for good.

As a young girl I had hung photographs and magazine and newspaper clippings of the models I emulated on my bedroom wall. I was such a typical child, and my dreams were much like any normal American girl. As I matured in my faith, those pictures and clippings would fade and one day be replaced with mental photographs of people such as Martha Myers, Bill Koehn and Kathy Gariety as well as all the humanitarian workers I met on my journey through the Middle East. Also added to that growing list of new heroes were Heather Mercer and Dayna Curry, two young women captured by the Taliban in 2001 while serving in Afghanistan. I prayed for them—and watched God provide a miracle when they were freed after three months. I saw in these two young ladies the same determined and loving spirit as that of our workers in Yemen. Even after such a frightening experience, they were both ready to go back and serve the people of Afghanistan.

In a day in which heroes are usually movie stars, rock stars and athletes, these missionaries rise far above the rest. I have come a long way since my youth. It is part of the change the Holy Spirit makes in our lives when we open up the chambers of our hearts to Him.

John Ashcroft was quoted recently on his opinion about the differences between Islam and Christianity: "Christianity is a faith in which God sends His son to die for you, while Islam is a religion in which Allah requires you to send your son to die for him."[9] These "heroes of the faith" were willing to take up the cross of Jesus and follow Him even unto death. What great examples of faith . . . Martha, Bill and Kathy. They died with dignity and honor. The Bible tells us in John 15:13, "Greater love has no one than this, that one lay down his life for his friends."

These three heroes loved the people of Yemen so much that they were willing to serve the peoples' medical and humanitarian needs even unto death. They had been born in the land of freedom and monetary wealth, yet they left those freedoms at the border to serve a needy people. My short time with them helped me see that freedom is a tremendous gift—and freedom in Christ is the best kind of freedom one can acquire.

I can hear the Father saying to them, "Well done, My good and faithful servants."

18

ROMANIACS FROM SOUTH CAROLINA

While I served as a trustee on the IMB, my father was continuing his trips to Romania. He worked with government leaders to develop a pastoral support system that brought hundreds of South Carolinians to Romania each year.

The Pastor Support System was a program of Laity Alive and Serving in which South Carolinians could help provide for a pastor in Romania. Many Romanian believers who had endured Communism now felt called by God to train as pastors, and through the Pastor Support System, Americans could give toward their training as well as toward the building of churches. The Romanian Christians contributed funds from their own pockets, as well, and supplied most of the labor to put up the church buildings. Romanian pastors were then placed in a newly built church and given financial help until the congregation could eventually support the pastor on their own. Many churches and Sunday school classes in South Carolina adopted pastors in an attempt to train and quickly place as many as possible. In a ten-year period, about fifty pastors were sponsored through this program.

Many Baptists from South Carolina became involved in helping pastors, building churches and doing social ministries. Some of those whom my father introduced to Romania were gifted people who became frequent short-term missionaries on their own initiative. Greg and Bobbie Horton, Jesse and Wilma Powers, John and Margie Simmons, and Jimmy and Peggy Morse were some of the couples who began to serve Romania through the ministries to which they were already attached.

Greg and Bobbie Horton, after first visiting Romania with my dad, returned to the country many times to help build churches and assist with the purchase of agricultural equipment. Greg and Bobbie were both touched from their very first visit, after which Greg proclaimed, "God spoke to our hearts about the great physical and spiritual needs of the Romanian people."

Greg, a former South Carolina Baptist State Convention president, and I proposed to the IMB that South Carolina Baptists partner with Romanian Baptists, since each state within the SBC adopts a country for special ministry focus and partnership every three years. Our request was granted, and the South Carolina Baptist Convention adopted the country of Romania for their ministry focus from 1998 to 2000. Sadly, before the Convention officially began its ministry to Romanians, Greg Horton died unexpectedly on February 18, 1997. His wife Bobbie was grieved but remained committed to the vision. A few months after his death, she returned to Romania to continue the work. Several years later, she remarried and brought her new husband to serve with her. Bobbie and Matt Caldwell still serve in Romania on a yearly basis.

South Carolinians from all over the state went to Romania during that three-year IMB endeavor, which ultimately involved 797 volunteers working with 404 churches. The volunteers conducted sports clinics, medical clinics, vacation Bible schools, ESL classes and the Experiencing God courses written by Henry and Richard Blackaby. According to Debbie McDowell, director of the South Carolina partnership with Romania, there were 2,246 professions of faith in Romania during that three-year period.

Jesse Powers was a former pastor and an evangelist. He and his wife Wilma had always done mission work in various parts of the world. His ministry to Romania, which has lasted for some sixteen years to date, will probably be marked as his most significant contribution to our Lord's work. Jesse is a sweet servant with a heart of gold, having the statesmanship of Senator Strom Thurmond and a preaching style like evangelist Junior Hill—simple and to the point. He has become a household name in the cities and villages of Cluj, bringing some fifty to one hundred people from the States each year to see and join in the work of preaching and of building churches.

John and Margie Simmons fell in love with Romania as soon as they saw it. After an early retirement from Bell South, John went straight into working for the Lord full time. Margie always went with him on his trips to Romania. John always handled all the planning of their trips and also coordinated large container shipments of supplies. He was the mastermind of logistics and details, and Margie took care of the relationships and social elements. Together they brought many friends and their entire family to Romania to get involved.

As devoted Presbyterian Church in America members, they brought many PCA Christians to Romania to help in church planting and ministry work among Baptists. To John and Margie, the differences between their denomination and ours were less important than the work that needed to be done. They counted themselves Christians first and Presbyterians second. They started a ministry called Christian Ministries International (CMI), which helps get containers of needed goods to Romania and to other countries in the world. Unfortunately, John died in April of 2008, but his unrelenting Margie continues to run the ministry. She returned to Romania just four months after his death.

Jimmy Morse was an evangelist and a preacher, and his wife, Peggy, was a nurse. In 1996 Jimmy and Peggy Morse packed their bags and moved to Romania. They helped coordinate many ministries, and they loved working in the orphanages. They became surrogate parents to many children in Dej, Romania, who didn't have families to care for them.

There were others, including Dr. Alastair Walker, pastor of First Baptist Spartanburg, and Dr. Benny Littlejohn, at that time pastor of Southside Baptist in Spartanburg, who raised money to help build much-needed churches in this formerly Soviet bloc country. Tom and Arlene Beal, lay people from Dr. Walker's church, eventually started a foundation called There is Hope which also helped build churches in the area outside Cluj.

A Meeting with the President of Romania

In May of 1991, my parents traveled to Romania, my mom for the first time, to meet with the first post-Communist president of Romania, Ion Iliescu. The president was trying to pull his country out of poverty, and he wanted my father's help to get a Most Favored Nation (MFN) status granted for Romania. Most Favored Nation status would allow Romania to enjoy lowered tariffs and reduction of trade barriers.

Romania had actually been given this status back in April of 1975 during Gerald Ford's presidency. In the mid 1980s, however, congressional criticism of Romania's deteriorating human rights records was increasing. In 1988, in an effort to preempt congressional action, Ceaușescu renounced MFN treatment, saying he felt the human rights requirements were unacceptable.

President Iliescu, however, knew his country needed this status to survive. He was willing to pay my father for his consultation and lobbying services. My father agreed to lobby President George H. Bush to reinstate MFN status to Romania—but he refused payment. My father wasn't interested in elevating a political leader for financial gain. He only desired a greater good, to help a people who had suffered so much. So instead of accepting financial remuneration for his services, he asked Ion Iliescu to promise Romanian Christians freedom of worship.

In 1992 my father paid a visit to then Secretary of State, James Baker. He lobbied Baker and made the case for Romania, recommending that they receive this MFN designation.

While they visited together, James Baker told my dad that

neither the State Department nor the CIA had predicted the fall of Communism. In Baker's words, "It was the hand of God." Should we be surprised that God is always in control and that He does as He wills for His purpose? Habakkuk 1:5 reads, "Look at the nations and watch—and be utterly amazed. For I am going to do something in your days that you would not believe, even if you were told."

James Baker reviewed the situation and eventually sent a deputy director to Romania to gather more information. In 1993 Congress restored the MFN status to the beleaguered country in recognition of her political and economic reform. My father, although not a government employee, was given the privilege of sharing with Romania the good news about the reinstatement. The news stations in the country filmed the event as his plane arrived in Bucharest. From the landing of the plane to the presentation of the papers, Romania's proud people and government leaders watched the much-anticipated event. In 1996 Romania received a permanent and unconditional extension of their MFN status.

The Romanian Christians had prayed for forty years, and God was answering their prayers through the American friends of the persecuted Romanians. During a trip I took there in 2008, the Romanians told me that President Iliescu had kept his word regarding religious freedom. In those early years after Communism, when the government had leaned toward restricting religious freedom, my father called to remind Iliescu of his promise. This was one more indication of my dad's desire to do all he could for these people who had endured so much rather than to elevate a leader or a party.

Time to Minister in Romania with My Dad

Since 1988 I had been active in my father's ministry, speaking with him and singing in churches and events where he was speaking. But I had never been able to work with him in Romania because of my role as a trustee of the IMB of the Southern

Baptist Convention between 1990 and 1998. With all the meetings I attended and the traveling I did for the board, besides attending to my job and my family, I had never had time to go overseas with my dad. That changed in January of 1998.

One night I woke up in the early morning hours and felt the Spirit of Lord telling me that it was time to be part of my dad's ministry in Romania. I sensed that the days were drawing near when he wouldn't be going there anymore. I shared the idea with my husband the next morning, and he agreed that I should go.

My first trip to Romania was in July of that year. It was wonderful speaking in churches across Romania with my dad and singing his favorite song, "People Need the Lord," which I learned to sing in the Romanian language.

I was impressed with the fervor and dedication of the Christians I met. It was a joy to meet the pastors who had endured so much and who had stood for their faith. I remember one of them, Benjamin Faragau, telling us about meeting several workers from the Navigators who had come to share the Bible and its teachings with them beginning in 1975. They had held secret meetings in the high grasses, using flashlights to study the Word of God, because they weren't allowed to distribute Bibles or Christian literature in Romania. I was amazed to see the very hymnbooks some of the devoted believers had hand copied still treasured in First Baptist Cluj.

Many of the pastors asked me what my father had been like before he was a Christian. I would jokingly say that he had been a little like some of their Communist leaders in that he did everything he could to stop me from following the Lord. The only difference was that he had done it because he loved me. Yes, he tried to stop me from following God's path, but he never beat me, imprisoned me or threatened me. Whenever I shared these things in meetings, my father always sat on the front row and would shout out, "It's true, every word of it—I was terrible!"

During the two weeks we were there, my father and I traveled from Oradea to Cluj, then to Braşov and on to Timişoara, and finally back to Budapest, Hungary, to fly home. It was such a joy to see the fruits of my father's labor from the past eight years. I met the ministers whom Laity Alive and Serving had helped train and the church buildings it had helped build. I saw the orphanages and social ministries that had been put in place. In Timişoara I remember my dad explaining what had happened during the revolution and showing me the memorial cross that now paid a tribute to those who had been gunned down during the Revolution.

It was such a wonderful experience. But almost every night when I went to bed, the Spirit of the Lord wouldn't allow me to sleep. He would bring to my mind all the things He had done for my father and my family. It was as if God was saying, "Do not forget what I have done for your family." I would cry myself to sleep, grateful for everything, and wondering where we would have been without the Lord. It was at this time that I began realizing that God was preparing me for bigger changes. I didn't know what they would be, but I knew they would involve my father.

When I got home to see my faithful husband, I shared with him my experiences as well as my fear that something was going to happen to Dad. Alton comforted me, reminding me how much the Lord had blessed us already and telling me how he too was grateful for what He had done in our lives. My father also would have been the first to say how much the Lord had blessed "this little boy from the little town of St. Matthews, South Carolina." He never ceased being grateful for all God had done in his life, and his ministry in Romania brought him great joy. Our Lord had been gracious to the Dent family.

19

THE UNEXPECTED TUNNEL

My father thought that the worst thing that could befall a person was to lose his mind. After we got back from Romania, things began to change, just as God's Spirit had warned me. In November of 1998, Dad went to the Mayo Clinic for a full physical. After many tests, they determined that he was fine—except that he was showing some mild cognitive impairment.

This would have been considered normal at my father's age; he was sixty-eight. But at the end of December 1998, he caught spinal meningitis and was hospitalized with a fever of 104 degrees. The family had known the symptoms of meningitis very well ever since my sister Dolly had contracted it at age twenty-two and nearly died. Meningitis is a life-threatening infection that inflames the meninges—the tough layer of tissue surrounding the brain and spinal cord.

Facing Facts

In July of 1999, my father was granted "Honorary Citizenship" by the city of Cluj. He was bestowed this honor for his social, medical, economic and educational work on behalf of the people there. This award is written in the Golden Book of Honor in the City Hall of Cluj. Pictures of the award ceremony still hang there. My sister, Dolly Montgomery, was able to be present with my dad when he received this award. Although Dad didn't know it, this would be the last time he would visit there.

In September of 1999, Dr. Frank Martin Jr. noticed Dad appeared to be jaundiced, and test results showed his bilirubin counts were abnormally high. These symptoms could be indicative of pancreatic cancer or, less seriously, a clogged bile duct. Dad was admitted for further tests. He subconsciously sensed his mind was slipping, and as such, if the tests showed he had pancreatic cancer, he felt ready to meet his Maker. But amazingly, the tests showed he had neither of the suspected medical conditions.

Just two months later, on Thanksgiving Day, my parents announced to the family that they would be moving to a retirement center called Laurel Crest. They said they would live in a patio home independently until they needed help. For some people this would seem like good news, but for me it signaled the beginning of the end. The announcement made it difficult for me to function at work or at home. That week after Thanksgiving was the most difficult of my life. The one thing I didn't want to do was watch my parents go downhill. The hard facts of life are that most of us will go through such a struggle, and the closer one is to the parent, the more painful that process will be to watch.

In January of 2000, my parents moved to Laurel Crest and gave away their library and mementos to Clemson University, the University of South Carolina and Columbia International University. It crushed me to see them give up their home. But my mother never looked back, except to say, "I'll never have to fix another commode, or get up on the roof, or worry about the yard." She had always taken care of all those sorts of details, and now she was preparing herself just to be able to help my dad if he needed it.

The month after my parents moved, our family threw a celebration in honor of Dad's seventieth birthday and my parents' forty-eighth wedding anniversary. We had a big barbecue dinner and roast at the First Baptist Church Columbia dining hall. I spent hours making a video for this event. I had to go through many old pictures, and the memories made me cry. I must have cried most of the time I was making the video. It reminded me how far we had come spiritually as a family and what the Lord had done in our lives. We roasted and toasted our parents with family and friends from all over the state of South Carolina, and my sister and I sang a duet for the first time to pay a tribute to them.

Although Senator Thurmond wasn't able to come, he sent a letter to be read at the dinner. In his normal joking manner, he exclaimed that he would be happy to be Harry's pallbearer one day. My father and the senator had a longstanding joke about who would have the last word at the other's funeral. They both claimed they would outlive each other. Jack Bass's book, *Ole Strom*, ends with the quandary of "who will be eulogizing whom?"[1] Thurmond had asked that Harry give his eulogy, "unless I have to give Harry's first," he said. Looking back at this celebration, I noticed that my highly spirited and vivacious father was more introverted and quiet than normal.

In September of 2000, my parents traveled to Washington to attend Julie Thurmond's marriage to Martin Whitmer at Washington National Cathedral. Although Julie's father was ninety-seven years old at the time, the senator proudly walked his daughter down that long aisle, taking small steps. It was one of those "mind over matter" things he was determined to do. My mom and dad were Julie's godparents and wouldn't have missed her wedding for anything.

The senator reminded my father at the Southern-style reception, which included a grits table, that he wanted him to preach his funeral service. The never-ending debate between two good friends continued. He also invited Dad to come up in May and spend a day with him for old times' sake. My father was anxious to visit with his mentor, so we made the plans ahead of time.

Changes, with Honors

My dad was a regular contributor for the *Times and Democrat*, a daily paper for which he wrote a column about faith, politics and character education. Shortly after returning from Julie's wedding, my mother and I noticed some problems in one of his articles. We began having to proof his writing before it was sent, as he was making mistakes he would not have normally made.

Dad was also still serving on the Executive Committee of the Southern Baptist Convention, as he had since 1996, and up to this time he had regularly traveled to Nashville for meetings. Mom and I discovered that he was starting to get lost while walking through the executive Baptist building—a place where he had formerly been quite at home. We were not sure how to handle the situation, as my father did not acknowledge what was happening. For a while my mother made sure that one of us always traveled with him to meetings. But soon we realized that he would no longer be able to serve, so we made a difficult decision and wrote a letter of resignation for him. It was at this time that we also had to take the car keys from him.

In the early part of 2001 my father was blessed with several honors. In January he and my older brother, Harry S. Dent Jr., received National Scouting Awards simultaneously. In the following month Dad received a second honor, the Character Education Award, from the South Carolina Department of Education for his work in character education. But the award my dad would treasure the most was given in March when the "forbidden place," a.k.a. Columbia International University, recognized him as the Alumnus of the Year. I made sure I was there to see the inspiring event. As I walked the campus, I remembered myself as a student some twenty-five years earlier. I never in a million years would have believed then that this day would come. God had a plan so unbelievable that at that time my mind could not have conceived it.

My mother accepted the alumnus award for Dad and made the acceptance speech to protect him from being confused in public. This was at the time when we were becoming unsure about what my dad might say if given the opportunity to speak in front of people. When CIU had first called my parents to tell them about the award, my mother had explained to them the changing situation, and they understood her need to help Dad out. It was a glorious day, and I am so glad my dad received the award when he was able to be aware of it.

In April, just a month after the special awards ceremony, my parents decided to go to Bermuda to attend a CIU-sponsored Bible study retreat where then President George Murray would be speaking. But after leaving the comfort and security of his home at Laurel Crest, Dad awakened in Bermuda completely disoriented. We immediately had to arrange to bring him back. It was a nightmare for my mom. We had also scheduled him to fly to Washington DC in May to spend the planned day with Senator Thurmond, but that trip had to be cancelled. We learned from this event that my father would never again leave the security of his home.

What's Wrong with Denial?

Life was changing for the Dent family. Taking care of Harry became a full-time job for my mom and my sister Dolly. I became the relief pitcher who drove the two hours every other weekend so my mom and sister could get away and get some sleep at night. We had seen enough to know that Dad wasn't the same, that he had some sort of mild dementia. My father was becoming increasingly confused as time went on. He was beginning to forget all the things he had done in life. When I visited him, I played the video I had made for his seventieth birthday party to remind him of some of the wonderful things he had accomplished.

One weekend when I was staying with him, he woke up and insisted I take him home to St. Matthews to see his mother. Frankly, I didn't know what to do since his mother had died some fifty years earlier. But I had learned earlier not to argue with him—it didn't work. So I drove him to his hometown to reminisce.

We enjoyed our day, seeing where he had grown up, and we visited some people he knew. Then I took him to his mother's grave. He looked at it, and it sparked the memory of her death. "Oh," he said, "I forgot she died." I didn't say anything more about it.

I couldn't help but notice how much he was retreating to his childhood days. In fact, he seemed obsessed with them. He would constantly reminisce about his two beloved brothers who had died in World War II. He would tell me the story of their service in the war and how they died, and then ten minutes later he would tell me the entire story again. I think I heard it about five times one day. I just acted as if each repetition was the first time.

At first, I tried to ignore the changes in my father. It was too painful admitting what was happening before my eyes. The one thing my father had never wanted to happen to him was happening, and there was nothing I could do to stop it. I was at the point where I could no longer deny what was occurring, nor could I excuse it as the normal process of aging.

Severe Cognitive Decline

As the beauty of spring came, we continued going through the dark tunnel. My father, the Energizer Bunny who had never been short of words, was having a hard time speaking in full sentences. We were getting down to two-word statements. We noticed, however, when we would ask him to pray, that he would say the most beautiful heartfelt prayers in complete sentences. He delighted in praying to his Lord.

In May of 2001, I had just returned from staying with my father for the weekend when I got a phone call in the wee hours of the night. Dad had awakened in the middle of the night and didn't know who my mother was. The confusion drove up his anxiety level, and it terrified my mother. When Dolly arrived to help, they called an ambulance because they thought he might be having a heart attack. I came to stay with him in the hospital the next night, and he had electrodes attached to his heart. Instead of a heart attack, it was found that he had undergone a major panic attack.

My father looked at me and said, "What's wrong with me? Is there something wrong with me?"

I replied, "There were just checking your heart, and it's fine."

"It needs to be my heart," he said with a sad tone.

I knew what he meant. There were times when he seemed to realize that he was losing his mind, and the pain of that was so unbearable to him that he usually blocked out the thoughts, just as I did. Deep inside, though, when he was honest about what was happening, he hoped a heart problem or some other physical ailment would take him home to heaven before any further mental deterioration took place. He was struggling to control himself as best he could, but his mind was short-circuiting in so many ways. It was beyond his control. That night he stayed up all night wandering the hospital floors; I followed behind him.

Later, when he was more coherent, I explained to him what had happened. He was devastated that he hadn't known who his precious Betty was. There was no one he loved more or wanted to protect more than his dancing girl. The thought that he wasn't in control of his mind and had actually frightened his precious wife was more than he could stand. It appeared to me that from this point on, he started turning inward, because he didn't want to do anything to hurt or scare her. Retreating into one's own world is a part of dementia. He was beginning to dance solo, oblivious to our desire to dance with him.

It was during that emergency stay at the hospital that we first heard the word *Alzheimer's*. Before that we had been told it was mild dementia and short-term memory loss—we didn't want to believe this new diagnosis. We held onto the idea that the changes were the natural result of aging. The alternative was too painful to bear.

Alzheimer's disease was first discovered in 1906 when Dr. Alois Alzheimer, a German neurologist, discovered the plaque on the brain of a woman who had died from dementia. Later, while doing research, I found that the beginnings of this disease start some thirty years before the first symptom.[2] Until recently patients with Alzheimer's disease were formally diagnosed during advanced stages of decline. It was the same in our situation—by the time we realized exactly what was happening, the degenerative brain disease had progressed considerably. These days, with superior MRI technology, Alzheimer's can be detected at earlier stages.

Things were changing rapidly. Dad's care was beginning to consume my heart-broken mother and my devoted sister during the week and me on the weekends. But with every flicker of pain piercing my broken heart, I remembered what the Lord had done for my father, and I was grateful.

Where Do We Draw the Line?

Our family has always gotten together for a beach vacation in July. The vacation of July 2001 was the last family vacation we had with all of us there. We had to set up a schedule to make sure my dad was monitored around the clock. During our vacation we sat down as a family to decide what to do about the situation with my father. We had been caring for him in his own home, but we sensed that the time was coming when he would need full-time care in a facility. As we talked, we decided we would keep him at home until he no longer knew who we were.

At the same time, we knew we had to protect Mom from going under. We had done enough research and heard enough stories to know what the stress of Alzheimer's can do to the main caretaker. As my brother Jack said, "Momma, we don't want to lose you too." July of 2001 was also the last time we took a family picture together with Mom and Dad, their children and spouses and all their perfect grandchildren. Our family beach vacation would never feel the same in later years without Dad.

We encouraged my mom to find a sitter for my father during the day. Then she and Dolly could take the shifts in the afternoons and at nights. I would continue coming every other weekend, and sometimes every weekend, to fill in. Our families sacrificed a lot by allowing Dolly and I to help Mom care for our dad. My mother's and sister's lives were totally consumed by the devastating effects of this illness. They would see it almost every day, and this meant they grieved the most. My brothers gave as much support as they could, but neither of them lived close enough to help with the round-the-clock care. In a sense, we were experiencing death in slow motion.

When I drove down to help on the weekends, I would leave from work and cry the whole way there and back. It was so painful to see Dad going downhill. There was never any good news, only further decline and more problems to deal with. My father loved to walk and see the outdoors, so we spent a lot of time walking and doing things he had never done before—like watching birds and nature. One day I showed him the video I had made of his life, and he didn't realize that he was the man in the video. When I would leave, he would give me a hug that felt distant. All this was extremely painful to see and experience, but I did not forget what the Lord had done for my father.

The Pressure Keeps Building

My father's decline came during a time of great stress in our lives. It started happening just after Alton and I had moved to Clemson for his new job as a professor of American Sign Language at Clemson University; I too had a new job as a counselor in the Oconee County schools. The difficulty we had encountered trying to selling our house in Spartanburg, resulting in our having to pay both a mortgage and rent, brought financial pressure. Our twin sons were adjusting to a new high school for their eleventh grade year. And we were missing our custom-built home, the church we had been members of for twenty years and our wonderful neighbors and friends.

The anxiety kept piling on—and then the attack of 9/11 happened. We were certainly at the high end of the stress calculator, and the strain of helping care for my father and watching him decline came on top of it all. It was a bit more than I could bear.

Two years of living in our one-thousand-square-foot apartment in Clemson, keeping up an unsold home in Spartanburg and caring for my dad in Columbia on the weekends started taking a toll. In one week, I would actually sleep in three different places. At times I would wake up confused as to where I was. There were days when it was so hard for me to get out of bed to go to work in the early morning that my husband had to massage my feet to get me going.

We decided not to think about the stress. It would only make things worse. We remembered the verse in First Corinthians, "No temptation has seized you except what is common to man. And God is faithful . . . he will also provide a way out so that you can stand up under it" (10:13). God would not fail us. The Bible promised us that He would not allow the testing to become too hard for us. When it came, He would make a way out so we could go through it.

When God provides a way out, it is His way of promising He won't give us more than we can handle. Yet we were beginning to wonder if we had made a mistake by moving. We fasted and prayed, asking God to show us if we had not followed His perfect will.

Later, in May of 2003, God gave us the certainty that we were within His will when Clemson University named my Alton Professor of the Year. We were shocked when the award was announced. In just three years' time, the students had chosen Alton for this prized recognition. God made it clear. We knew it was His way of encouraging us through the hard times.

Our twin sons came home one day after attending a Bible study and exclaimed to us, "We are being pruned." They were right, and the pruning hurt. My husband and I kept saying, "As long as our boys are doing well and we're all healthy, we can make it." We began to be thankful for the simple things in life, like the facts that we had a roof over our heads, clothes on our backs and food to eat. Most importantly, we had each other.

We simplified our life into three main goals: making sure our sons got what they needed to succeed, taking care of my parents and just keeping our heads above water. Even getting settled and established in our new community was not one of our priorities. That would have to wait. But even as my stomach was churning from all the upheaval in our lives, I did not forget what the Lord had done for my father.

My Parents Celebrate Their Fiftieth Anniversary

In August of 2001, my mother took my father to the USC Medical School in Charleston for an evaluation. The Alzheimer's expert, Dr. David Bachman, was amazed at how quickly my father's mind had degenerated. There are six stages to Alzheimer's. Normally it takes a person eight to fifteen years to pass through all six stages, but our Harry passed through them in just three. We barely had time to adjust to each stage. The doctors wondered if the rapid progression of this disease was due to the meningitis, which had inflamed his brain with a high fever.

Needless to say, when my parents' fiftieth wedding anniversary rolled around, Dad didn't even know. It was the first year in all their married life that he didn't acknowledge it, so the kind doctors at the hospital sent my mother flowers.

Dad had come to the point at which he could no longer call any of us by name, nor could he even recognize a picture of himself. There were times when he even saw us as imposters or enemies. He began having delusions and hallucinations. I learned to have a sense of humor and just "go with the flow." If he saw something that was not there and it frightened him, I just told him that I'd taken care of it and it was gone. We learned not to argue with him, because it only made things worse. Sometimes I would take Dad for a ride when he was bothered by something.

When we got back, he had forgotten what was bothering him.

I'll never forget the day he came out of his room with my mother's jeans and shirt on. Taking care of him was so much like dealing with a young child. The doctors in Charleston were amazed we had been keeping him at home through all the stages. They told us we should be looking for a place to take care of him before a major emergency happened. But just then that was just too hard for our hearts to ponder. My mother, sister, brothers and I were all filled with grief, but I did not forget what the Lord had done for my father.

ONGOING CHANGES
AND
CHALLENGES

Many years ago I had promised the Lord that if He would bring my father to know Him, I would not be angry when it was time for Dad to die. As painful as things now were, I was determined to keep my promise. I had not forgotten what the Lord had done for my father and my family, but I wondered what He was trying to teach us through all this.

The Medical University of South Carolina sponsored a convention on Alzheimer's in 2002, and my mother and I were invited to come and participate. I was eager to learn everything I could about this disease. While my sister, Dolly, was reading books just trying to keep up with the stages and how we should handle each one, I wanted to know why this had happened to my father, and why it was happening to so many Americans. The meeting included some of the top medical research scientists and doctors from the university and from around the US, and I didn't shy away from asking questions.

I learned very quickly that Alzheimer's disease is not necessarily a disease of old age. As with cancer, people are more likely to get it as they get older, but some have been subjected to it when as young as forty. The disease itself is caused by a plaque that forms on the cells of the brain due to a weakened immune system (at the convention we saw a slide of this Alzheimer's-inducing plaque, now able to be viewed by experts due to medical advancements). The main reason we are more likely to develop Alzheimer's as we get older is simply because our immune systems weaken with age.

In addition to the aging factor, our immune systems are weakened by toxins in our bodies—and the level of toxins in our culture is on the rise. There are increasing numbers of free radicals (unstable atoms and molecules which can damage cells) getting into our systems though what we drink, breathe and eat. Our bodies are made to throw off a certain amount of toxins, but it is increasingly more difficult to eject them at the rapid rate they are entering our bodies.

I also learned that once Alzheimer's starts, it's very difficult to stop.

Heredity or Environment?

Some of the answers to my questions were alarming. I asked the researchers to compare the number of people with Alzheimer's in the United States per capita to the numbers in other countries. They told me that "we in the US have more people proportionately with this disease than all other groups." The workshops I attended emphasized the role of culture and environment over the role of heredity with this disease.

Dr. Jacobo Mintzer, a neurologist and psychiatrist from the Medical University of SC, remembers the day that a new drug called Tegretol promised symptomatic relief for Alzheimer's patients. "Although the last ten years have been marked by false hopes and disappointments, thanks to the joint efforts of the government, the private sector and the public, we are now able to detect signs of Alzheimer's disease before the first memory deficits are present." He also said, "Although a cure was once the hope of the past, prevention seems to be the goal for the future."[1]

According to the Alzheimer's Research and Prevention Foundation (ARPF), "Memory loss can be prevented by lifestyle choices that incorporate an integrative approach to brain fitness and longevity."[2] Other research scientists, including Dr.

Dharma Singh Khalsa (president of the ARPF), also feel that prevention is the best way to fight this terrible disease. Prevention, according to Dr. Khalsa, includes daily rigorous exercise, diet and nutrition, stress management and pharmaceuticals.[3] The best diet for this offensive approach includes lots of fresh fruits and green vegetables—which provide anti-oxidants and phyto-chemicals—and low-cholesterol foods. In a nutshell, our processed, fast-food, hydrogenated, chemical-laden diets and lack of exercise are the main culprits.

In *The Anti-Alzheimer's Prescription Book*, Dr. Vincent Fortanasce calls this disease the Great American Epidemic.[4] I came to call it the black plague of America. Dr. Fortanasce is a well-respected neurologist who lost his own father to this dreaded disease. He noticed that people in highly stressful jobs were most likely to get this disease—people such as CEOs, executives, doctors, attorneys and politicians. He also realized in 2001 that the histories of his Alzheimer's patients had three things in common: poor quality of sleep, unpredictable stress and a lack of exercise and relaxation.[5] Dr. Fortanasce's work meticulously analyzes the current research, revealing that Alzheimer's disease could be prevented in 70 percent of patients and delayed ten to fifteen years in those patients genetically predisposed to the disease.[6]

Reading his book made me think about my father, Ronald Reagan and Carroll Campbell (the former governor of South Carolina), all of whom had been victims of the disease. My father's career in politics, especially during the Thurmond and White House days, involved sixty- to eighty-hour workweeks and being on call twenty-four hours a day. It has been said that high stress causes heads of state to age two to three years for every year in office.

I couldn't help but notice that George H.W. Bush, Bill Clinton and George W. Bush were avid daily joggers. Exercising must have been their way of relieving stress. I learned from reading Dr. Archibald Hart's book *Adrenaline and Stress* that living in a constant state of high alert leads to premature death. Simply said, our bodies weren't meant to live off a perpetual adrenaline rush.[7]

I examined my husband's and my eating habits and found that we were eating slightly better than the average American. But slightly better wasn't good enough. We Americans have basically inverted the food pyramid. We live by what tastes good instead of the way the Lord intended us to eat. My husband and I began gradually to increase the healthiness of our diets, and we both began to exercise more. We also started drinking more clean water. Everything Senator Thurmond had taught me as a child was beginning to come back to my mind: "Don't eat too much junk food, exercise daily and drink lots of clean water." I only wished I had listened to him sooner.

There have been many times when I have been on a treadmill at a gym and found the person next to me was there because they also had a parent with Alzheimer's. Fear is a great motivator.

When my sons Jonathan and Harrison were working as pages for ninety-eight-year-old Senator Thurmond, my husband and I went one day to pick them up. The senator was then experiencing short-term memory problems and having a hard time keeping our sons' names straight. But when he saw me, that long-term memory kicked in. I tried to explain to him what had happened to my father and why he hadn't been able to come and spend another day with him as he had requested. Considering his own age and generally sharp mental faculties, the senator couldn't understand why my dad would not have his.

"You were right, Senator," I said.

"Right about everything?" he replied.

"Not everything, Senator, but many things. You were right about everything you tried to teach me about eating good fruits and vegetables, exercising, getting plenty of sleep and drinking lots of good, clean water. I just wish I had listened sooner."

That was the last time I would see Strom Thurmond in person. What memories it brought to my mind just to be in his office again. His office staff and the atmosphere itself always made me feel at home. I'm happy my sons were able to share part of my experiences, even if just for a month as pages.

A Heartrending Decision

My father loved to walk in his later years. As his mind continued to deteriorate, he and I would often walk down by the riverfront near Laurel Crest and sit in the rocking chairs there. To get down to the riverfront, we had to walk by Laurel Crest's nursing-home wing. My father would say, "I don't ever want to go there."

But as time went on, my father passed through all the declining stages of the mind with this terrible disease. Going through the stages was like passing through a dark tunnel, and we were desperately looking for a light at the end. Whenever we thought we could catch a glimpse of a light, it always proved to be another dreaded stage coming.

Families who are going down the track with this horrifying disease never get any good news. It only gets worse with time. There's no remission, as there can sometimes be with cancer. We were caught in a cycle of grief we could not escape. And that cycle usually brings depression with it. I had never experienced that feeling until this illness with my father. Now Dad's brain was affecting the rest of how his body functioned, and the pain of it cut deep into my soul.

Despite Dad's desire, we knew the moment had come to find a full-time care facility. He no longer knew who we were, although he did sometimes seem to notice a familiarity about us—especially my mother. But Mom, who'd already had one major back surgery and now had arthritis, could no longer care for him. Mom, my sister and I were all reaching the point of exhaustion. It was becoming difficult to lift Dad and to assist him with the necessities of life. My sister and mother went all over town looking for the best place for our precious Harry, and their research took us to Still Hopes in West Columbia.

It's agonizing to think about putting a loved one in full-time care. As a family, we decided together in February of 2002 to transfer Dad to a retirement facility, Still Hopes, which offered special care to people with Alzheimer's. Now, instead of us taking care of Dad full time with some assistance from others, a highly trained staff would be caring for him around the clock with our assistance.

Just because you have full-time care for a person doesn't mean you no longer take care of that person. Once we moved Dad into his new home, my mother went to see him almost every day. My sister helped as much as she could, and I visited every time I could get to town. It was a painstaking job just making sure he got what he needed.

Leaving my dad there for the first time was very troubling. My sister and mom had that tough job. I was getting ready to leave for a convention the day after he was placed at Still Hopes, and before I left I went with my mom to see him. Mom and I put our arms around each other and wept. We had hoped this day would never come, and the realization and the pain were unbearable. I sobbed all the way to my convention at Hilton Head Island. When I arrived, I sat right next to a retired counselor who intuitively sensed something was bothering me. She took me aside and asked, "Is everything all right?"

I told her what my family had just done and why. She said her mother had died from Alzheimer's, and she had also had to put her in a full-time care facility. "You will see, in time," she said, "that you did the right thing—even though it hurts now." And she was right.

Several months later, an orthopedic surgeon told my mother that she needed major back surgery. We found out that if she had moved the wrong way during the many months she had been handling my dad, she could have been paralyzed for life. We were grateful to have this problem identified before any serious injury took place. So, two months after we placed my father at Still Hopes, my mother went in for surgery. During those days I would leave one hospital, where I had been spoon-feeding my mother because she could not lift her head, and then go over to my dad's to make sure he was spoon-fed as well. At least my mother's condition was temporary, although she had a painful recovery ahead of her.

I continued to go to Columbia quite often, not only to visit my dad but also to be a help to my mom. My sister was a daily support to both of our parents. There were times when Dad had a good moment and seemed to recognize us by the look in his eyes; we just seemed familiar to him. Don't ever doubt that you should visit someone who is in this condition, because they are still human beings with feelings. They can sense it when others care about them, even though the communication is a one-way street. And they seem at times to respond to human touch.

I can remember one day walking with Dad in the courtyard, and he looked me straight in the eye and said, "Sing." I knew what he meant. That one word meant, "Sing my favorite song, and you know what it is." So I sang the song I had performed in ministry with him in Romania and all over South Carolina: "People Need the Lord." I decided not worry about who was watching and listening. When he heard the song, his whole face lit up.

Another day he seemed very alert and was trying to communicate with me. I asked him, "Am I one of your favorite daughters?" He responded by saying, "You better betcha!" There were times when I knew he wanted to tell us something, but his mind was too confused to be able to communicate. Instead, he responded with blinks and occasionally a short word or two. Sometimes I just spoke to him as if nothing had changed and as if he understood what I was saying, although I never knew whether he did or not.

The Senator Passes at 100

Our dear friend Senator Thurmond finally lost his race with my dad when he passed away in June of 2003. When the senator died, I brought my dad a picture of the senator and told him that his friend had passed on at age one hundred. He didn't appear to respond or to know who I was talking about. I also informed him that his grandsons Jonathan and Harrison had served as pages to the senator the summer before. Again, no response.

Nonetheless, I went on to tell him about everything that had happened at Senator Thurmond's funeral, including the bagpipes playing *Amazing Grace* at the end and the eulogy that was given by then Senator Joe Biden from Delaware. Even though the rain was pouring on the day he died, well-wishers stood inside and outside First Baptist Church, which was filled to capacity. It was so eerie attending the senator's funeral and realizing that the missing piece was my father's presence. I told my dad every detail about the more than two-hour tribute to his good friend, despite his lack of response.

The senator's doctor signed his death certificate, stating that he "simply died of old age." Rarely is a doctor able to write that these days. All the senator's discipline in eating a healthy diet, drinking water, getting plenty of exercise and maintaining good sleep habits had paid off.

Essie Mae Washington-Williams Steps Forward

When my father, back in 1998, had read Jack Bass's book *Ole Strom*, he was stunned. He and I were on our way to speak together at a church conference retreat when he earmarked a page and told me to read that chapter. I still have the scratch paper on which he wrote, "Read this, Ginny. Could it be true?" It was the chapter in which Jack Bass and Marilyn Thompson wrote about the senator's "colored offspring." My father knew Jack Bass to be a reputable author who would not print something he had not researched well; however, the allegation was just too hard to believe.

About six months after the senator's death, Essie Mae Washington-Williams stepped forward to announce that she was the daughter of Senator Thurmond. My first thought was, *Who is this woman making such ridiculous slander after all these years?*—

and then I saw her face in *The State* newspaper. *Oh my goodness*, I thought, *she looks just like the senator's sister Gertrude*. I immediately knew she was telling the truth. It was a shock to my entire family and to all of the senator's staff. It was a complete shock to his wife and children as well.

How could he have kept a secret like this for so long? I had known that a rumor about Strom Thurmond and his black daughter had been circling in the black communities of South Carolina for many years. These rumors dated back to Essie Mae's days at South Carolina State University. No one knew, however, exactly who his daughter was.

Part of me was disillusioned. This grandfather figure, whom I had admired all my life, had let me down. The other part of me was amazed at the chances he had taken in making sure Essie Mae was well cared for. Many people would have resorted to a quiet abortion to hide their sins. Or he could have given her up for adoption, which would have closed the case, and no one would have to know who the real father or mother was. It appeared to me that the senator had definitely failed in his moral standards, yet he had not failed in his moral obligations. I was amazed when I read Essie Mae's book *Dear Senator: A Memoir by the Daughter of Strom Thurmond* and found that he had actually encouraged her to come to South Carolina State University when he was running for governor—and that he had paid for her expenses.[8] What risks he took to ensure her needs were met and her potential developed.

In the end, I admired Essie Mae Washington-Williams for keeping the secret and Senator Thurmond for his desire to meet her needs. I only wish he had told his family and his constituents the truth long before he died. Frankly, the stress of keeping a secret like that would have caused me to die an early death. So I told my father about the senator's long hidden secret coming to light, and I even showed him the picture of Essie Mae. As usual, he didn't respond.

It was so foreign to me for my father not to respond to these things. He had spent his life as the closest confidant of Senator Thurmond, and it was sad to have him totally unresponsive now that he had finally won their race. But such is the heart wrenching pain of this disease. Each time he failed to acknowledge his family and friends, I would smile on the outside—but on the inside, I was dying. Oh, how I longed to converse with my dad just like we used to.

21

UPS
AND
DOWNS

During the summer of 2002, my husband and I drove to Washington DC to visit our sixteen-year-old boys while they worked for Senator Thurmond. On the way to the magical city of my childhood, we heard the shocking news on the radio that the constitutionality of having the words "under God" in the Pledge of Allegiance was being challenged in the courts of California. The Ninth Circuit held that public schools could not say the Pledge of Allegiance because the use of the words "under God" violated the establishment clause of the First Amendment.

Although we had been warned that such a day might come, it was too hard to believe that this was happening in our beloved America. My twin sons were working in the Senate when the senators, thankfully, voted unanimously to disapprove what the court had ruled. It was an important day in our country's history.

But the next day would puzzle us even more. Alton, my sons and I all attended the confirmation hearings of a dear friend of my family, Dennis Shedd, for a federal judgeship on the US Court of Appeals for the Fourth Circuit. No one will find a finer American than Dennis. He grew up in Cordova, South Carolina, and worked his way through college and law school. During his years at USC law school, he clerked for my father. My dad had admired him greatly. Now Dennis was in the fight of his life trying to get this confirmation.

I watched as Senator John Edwards and Senator Charles Schumer vigorously questioned Dennis about every aspect of his life. Their inquiry was so detailed that they might as well have inquired about which cartoons influenced him as a child. I'll never forget what I heard that day on June 27, 2002. Keep in mind that this was the day after the Senate had voiced their disapproval of the court's handling of the "under God" case in California. Charles Schumer looked at Dennis and said, "So you believe that the right to privacy, as embodied in the Constitution, would support a woman's right to choose?" He was needling him to see if he passed the litmus test of approving abortion. Schumer continued, "We have found people end up interpreting the law and it ends up being consistent with their views. . . . So to me it is not exactly accurate to say there is just some interpretation of the law apart from ideology that is divined as we priests of the law divine it."[1] Basically, he was pointing out that we all see things through the lens of our own beliefs—and thereby discounting whatever Dennis's response might be.

My memory of Schumer's words and intent seems to be, "I don't want to put a man on this court who looks to God for answers." However, after I ordered the written transcript, the words that I remember were not in it. Since my husband and I both heard similar words from Schumer, I wondered if someone had edited the transcripts.

Dennis was a churchgoing man who had lived his faith throughout his life. This is what Mother Teresa always advocated. The irony of it all shocked me into realizing how much this country had changed since our forefathers wrote the Constitution many years ago. Although our founding fathers believed that the State should not *establish* religion, they would never have confirmed a man to a court who did not profess a belief in God.

I spoke with Dennis afterward and later prayed for him. It was another six months before he finally received confirmation. He was only one of many judges President George W. Bush had difficulty getting approved. In fact, Bush was having difficulty with all his judicial appointments. There is something wrong with this country when a man like Dennis Shedd, who has received the American Bar Association's top rating, has trouble getting confirmed to a US governmental position. He had difficulty because he respects the Constitution and believes in interpreting it rather than rewriting it.

I've never forgotten Charles Schumer's statement to Dennis that day. I was amazed that not even one of the many reporters attending that day communicated Schumer's astounding revelation and that part of what we remembered was not contained in the actual transcript. It was then that I realized just what George Bush was up against as president, and I began to pray for him more diligently.

When I got back to Columbia, I recounted the entire ordeal to my dad, but he did not respond. He had fought so hard to keep the court from going to the left and to keep judges from being appointed who would rewrite the Constitution.

Things are changing in America and we are moving toward moral relativism, but who is noticing?

One Burden Lifted

Finally, in August of 2003, after three years of having our home in Spartanburg on the market, the house sold. During these years we had been living in a holding pattern, like a plane circling, waiting to land. We were both financially and physically exhausted from constant commuting and the keeping up of two households. This experience cured me from ever wanting two homes!

We were finally freed from the stress of it all, and that was a welcome freedom to have. In one week we moved out of our Clemson apartment into a condo, moved everything from our Spartanburg family home into storage and moved our twins into college. I never wanted to pack or move a box again. In January of 2004, we finally began building our home in the Seneca/

Clemson area. Meanwhile, we were still on the road going back and forth to Columbia to visit my dad and be a support to my mom.

Yes, one burden had been lifted. But there was more to come.

Another Jolt

In March of 2004, I got another jolt. A routine preventative blood test of my husband's showed that his PSA (prostate specific antigen) levels were just a little high. We'd been slowly changing our diet and increasing our health, but with this news, the doctors recommended a biopsy.

Alton wasn't fond of the idea. Being a good wife, I simply cried until he gave in. I was already losing my dad, and I didn't want to take any chances on losing my husband too. So in April we went for the biopsy. Neither one of us thought anything would come of it. After all, he had been an athlete most of his life and had always been healthy. In twenty-six years of work, he had only taken one sick day.

While I was already reeling from watching my dad go downhill and seeing what it was doing to my mom, I got the shocking news. My husband had prostate cancer.

We simply walked around in disbelief for a few weeks, telling no one. I remembered hearing, on my trip to the Middle East back in 1997, that King Hussein had sought help at Johns Hopkins for his prostate cancer. So I figured what was good enough for the king was good enough for my husband. To Johns Hopkins we went. Still numb, I asked one of hospital's world-renowned surgeons what could possibly have caused this cancer. I will never forget his answer: "The American diet is rubbish," he said, "and if we don't make some changes soon, there won't be a man left standing who does not have this cancer." It was becoming a common refrain, all this talk about the American diet and what it is doing to us.

Alton was scheduled for surgery later that summer. It would be a risky surgery, and he would have a lengthy recovery.

One day my husband woke up and said to me, "Honey, I'm not ready for this surgery. I will change my diet and do anything." So we started looking for the anything. We started eating every green thing in sight, and we consulted several naturopathic doctors. We read everything we could about prostate cancer, and we continued consulting with the medical doctors. Johns Hopkins, and later Emory, both told us that we had some time and that the new diet could make a difference. We just had to find out.

Alton's PSA score began to come down, which was a good sign—but it was coming down very slowly, and the dropping score didn't completely prove that the cancer was gone. Fearing we might be waiting dangerously long for treatment, we scheduled surgery again at Johns Hopkins some six months later. The ups and downs of fighting the battle against cancer—and not knowing its status—had gotten to us.

A Double Rainbow Appears

I wanted it all to be over. I wanted the cancer surgically removed, and I wanted to hear the surgeon say, "It's all gone and hasn't spread, and everything's going to be okay." It was Christmastime, and the present I most wanted was to hear those words of comfort and relief. So when my husband cancelled the surgery for a second time, I was heartbroken.

We packed our bags to go home to Columbia for Christmas. I really did not want to go. I was just not up to seeing my dad in his present state, and the fear of my husband's cancer had gotten the best of me. I resisted getting into the car, so my twin sons and my husband led me into the car as if I was the child. I just started to sob. The grief, worry and pain I was experiencing was consuming me. I felt helpless, and I was losing hope. Yes, this unsinkable Molly Brown was treading water and drowning in a wave of depression. After years of helping children and adults survive against the sinking abyss of depression, I was now falling prey to its clutches. *Could this be happening to me?* I realized, for the first time in my life, that I was not immune to the dreaded D word.

About an hour before we got to Columbia, we saw the most beautiful and unusual site I'd ever seen. After a violent storm, we all saw an amazing double rainbow! It was so enormous that it covered the expanse of the sky. I had never seen a full rainbow before, much less a double rainbow. My son Harrison said, "Mom, quit worrying. God is trying to tell you that everything is going to be all right." I believed my son was right, and his encouragement gave me a sense of comfort that day when I felt my whole world was falling apart. God spoke through my son and a double rainbow.

We continued making changes for a healthier lifestyle. We walked briskly on a daily basis to keep my serotonin levels elevated and fight against depression. We worked diligently to lower my husband's PSA levels. His levels had skyrocketed because of an infection he had gotten after his biopsy, but little by little they were coming down again.

After one year of dogged determination, we were within striking distance of reaching our goal of getting his PSA under 4.0. Even our doctors were amazed. My husband's lifelong allergies had gone away, and the infection he had gotten from the biopsy, which no doctor had been able to cure, was finally healed.

Then, just as our hopes were beginning to rise, Alton was working in the yard one day when he was attacked and stung repeatedly by a swarm of yellow jackets. This caused his PSA levels to rise a third time. That is when the doctors told us we now had to have the surgery. Fortunately for us, a doctor in Atlanta, Dr. Scott Miller, had just perfected what is called the da Vinci Surgical System. It was a minimally invasive, robotic, laparoscopic method which was proving highly successful in reducing the possible side effects of removing the prostate.

Although Dr. Miller had a waiting list of six to eight weeks, as well as many doctors coming to train under him, my husband, who was not on his list of patients, was allowed in and set up for surgery within a week's notice. Dr. Miller wondered how we had gotten on his surgery schedule when he'd never met us before. But I knew, because I had prayed for an opening.

During Christmas of 2005, Alton and I spent our thirtieth wedding anniversary at Northside Hospital in Atlanta, Georgia. After a grueling six-hour surgery, I was finally able to hear the words I had longed to hear: "Everything is all right . . . the cancer has not spread." A complete examination of the tissue showed that nothing had gotten worse in eighteen months. However, the prostate had definitely needed to be removed.

We learned something valuable through this experience: it's easy to get cancer—and getting it doesn't happen overnight. Cancer is the result of many years of improper habits, diet and stress. Once it starts, it's hard to cure just by changing one's diet. I am not saying it is impossible, but it is difficult. Besides adjusting our habits, an invention of modern medicine helped us. But ultimately, we know for sure that the Lord answered our prayers for healing through this surgical invention.

Today one of the topics I speak on is health and wellness. It wasn't that we were the best examples—but we learned so much the hard way that we were able to pass on our knowledge to others. I produced a DVD that is being used in some public schools in South Carolina called "The Basics of Life." It shows how we all need to get back to the basics of eating whole foods, staying hydrated, exercising, handling stress and getting plenty of rest. Somehow, we have missed the basics, but I learned them through researching Alzheimer's and through our journey with cancer.

Alton and I knew one thing for sure: we were willing to change our lifestyle as a preventative measure against cancer and Alzheimer's. We felt these two painful experiences were teaching us something. And we were weary of learning lessons the hard way.

22

OF TUNNELS AND LIVING WATER

On June 4, 2005, I got a call from Dolly saying that Dad had fallen into a deep sleep. My husband and I were out of town at the time, and I was told to get ready to come home, as they didn't expect Dad to wake up. Alton and I immediately returned and got ready to go to Columbia. I had what I call "double-dip feelings"—I was feeling two different things at the same time. One part of me was drenched in sadness, and the other part was leaping for joy at the prospect of Dad going home and, as he would call it, "finally graduating to heaven."

As we were leaving for the drive to Columbia, I got another call. Dad had awakened as if nothing had happened. After all, he was the Energizer Bunny.

The next morning, Ronald Reagan, our fortieth president, died after his own long bout with Alzheimer's. I watched the entire ordeal on television. My heart pounded when I saw his body lying in state in the Capitol Rotunda. It reminded me of when my father had taken me to the rotunda to see John F. Kennedy's casket. I felt such a deep sadness that I could not stop crying.

Then there was a beautiful service at the Washington National Cathedral, attended by many former presidents and world leaders such as Mikhael Gorbachev, Tony Blair and the interim presidents of Iraq and Afghanistan. Eulogies were given by Margaret Thatcher and several presidents of other countries. My heart went out to the Reagan family and especially to Nancy Reagan. I knew her pain. It was so hard for me to watch her every move when I knew almost exactly what she was feeling.

My father had worked closely with Ronald Reagan. These two Republicans had shared many of the same values and philosophies and, later, the same dreaded disease. After intensely watching the entire week of ceremonies, I was physically and emotionally exhausted.

What I felt were empathy and gratitude. Reagan had been such a supporter of the right to life, a supporter of a strong national defense, a states' rights advocate, an opponent of any kind of racial discrimination and a true conservative—and he had held one of the highest approval ratings of any president in US history. He himself had stated, "Our Founding Fathers knew a government couldn't control the economy without controlling the people." The more control given to a government (including control of the economy), the more control that government has over its people.

I have often wondered why my father chose Nixon and then Ford over this man. Then it hit me. God is ultimately in control, and He had chosen Reagan to be president at just the right time in history. The US hostages in Iran were released as Reagan was giving his inaugural address. After his assassination attempt, he himself believed that God had spared him for a greater purpose. In 1983, Reagan himself predicted the fall of Communism—and his prediction came to pass six years later. In 1984, he was reelected with a landslide victory, winning forty-nine of fifty states, and his second term would be blessed by the ending of the Cold War after summits with Gorbachev. Margaret Thatcher credited him with "winning the cold war for liberty without a shot being fired." Many people believed he was the major contributor to the collapse of the Communist walls. In my opinion, the timing of his presidency was clearly the hand of God, and He used Ronald Reagan to accomplish His purpose.

Although his beloved wife Nancy urged Congress and President George W. Bush to support federal funding for embryonic stem cell research, I don't believe Ronald Reagan would have supported that, even knowing the fate that lay before him. And my dad would have felt the same way. Of course my father and Ronald Reagan both wanted to spare their precious wives from what Alzheimer's would do to them—Nancy Reagan never could imagine living life without her "Ronnie," just as my mother never could imagine living life without her "Harry." But I feel, as I believe my dad and Reagan did, that we should fight this disease with prevention, not the harvesting of innocent embryos. If I have learned anything as a result of what my own family has gone through, it's that this horrible disease can be arrested by prevention. As it is said, an ounce of prevention is worth a pound of cure—and an unborn baby has a right to life.

The next time I saw my father, I told him that his friend Ronald Reagan had died. I watched for his response, but he gave me a blank stare. My father seemed to have lost all connection with his political past. He sometimes responded to hymns and to memories of his ministry—especially his work in Romania. It was as though the start of his new life in Christ was where his memories began.

Character Education Legacy Continues

In October of 2005, my sister Dolly was inducted into the town of Chapin's Hall of Fame for her volunteer work in promoting character education and for being the driving force in their "Community of Character" initiative. My mother, brothers and I were all there to celebrate the event. The ceremony brought tears to my eyes because the person who would have been the most delighted didn't even know what was going on that day. Dad would have been so proud if he could have been there. The next year, the school where I worked was one of ten nationwide to receive the Chick Fil-A Character Education Award.

I told my father of these accomplishments when I visited him the day my school won its award. I wanted him to know the legacy was continuing, but again, he didn't know what was going on. The legacy continued without his knowledge of it.

The Tunnel Gets Darker

As time went on, Dad's facial expression and blinks became fewer and fewer. There were times he didn't even notice we were in the room, or that we were holding him in our arms. Since the brain controls the rest of the body, and his was deteriorating, his body was beginning to go downhill. In just a few years, he had wasted away to a little over one hundred pounds. With his skin sagging between his bones, my dad was weak and frail.

It became increasingly harder to visit him without completely breaking down. We always had a family member, or on occasion a friend, feed him his main meal of the day. Otherwise, he tended not to eat as well. We asked our mother several times not to go every day because the grief was tearing her up. But she never listened to us, and she continued visiting almost every day, no matter how sad it made her. It was part of the commitment and devotion my parents had to each other.

The Missing Guest at the Wedding

It is such a joy to see your children find their lifelong partner. Back in 2004 Josh, our oldest, brought Sydney Swails to our home to meet us. What had started as a friendship between the two of them had blossomed into romance. Josh told us before he brought her to our home that she was the one.

We took a chance and brought Sydney to meet Harry at Laurel Crest so we could get his approval. We explained that she was Joshua's bride-to-be and asked Dad if he was happy with the plans. This time we got a response of "Uh huh!" Sydney didn't realize it, but she had made a big impression.

Josh and Sydney were married at Pawley's Island Baptist Church in October 2005 by an Episcopal minister and friend of our family, Rev. John Burley. As Joshua came to the front of the church to wait for his bride and Sydney started down the aisle, I had those double-dip feelings again. I was overjoyed, but I also wanted to cry because my daddy wasn't there to celebrate this special event with us. Whether at the rehearsal, the wedding itself or the reception, Harry's absence overshadowed the celebration. At the reception it was wonderful to dance with my son and my husband. But I wanted to reach out and dance with my dad once again, and he was not there. It would have been easier for me if I could have pictured my dad looking down from heaven rather than imagining him sitting in his nursing home room unaware of what was happening.

We finally realized that the only thing that gave him any sense of comfort or joy, besides seeing our somewhat familiar faces, was hearing Christian music or the mention of his ministry in Romania. So we brought a CD player into his room to play his favorite hymns, and we prayed with him and spoke of our Lord often.

Although faint, it was clear that the living water that had entered Dad at the age of forty-eight was still there. As Jesus promised His followers in the Gospel of John, "Whoever drinks the water I give him will never thirst. Indeed, the water I give him will become in him a spring of water welling up to eternal life" (4:14). We were so thankful that Dad had drunk from that living water, and we had no doubts about where he would go when he died. I will never forget what God did for my dad or what He did for my family, and I have thanked Him for it every day.

As the Harry we knew continued to fade and die, we became more willing for him to go home to his heavenly Father. His mind and body were deteriorating so much that the thought of heaven was a relief. We actually prayed that God would take him home quickly. We were longing for the day when his suffering would end. Just imagining what heaven would be like for him, as opposed to what he was going through, gave us great comfort.

The Final Call

On Tuesday night, September 25, 2007, I received a call from my mother saying that my father was close to death and only expected to live a few more days. By the time I got to Columbia the next day, he wasn't expected to live through the night. I would stay the night with him. The nursing home kindly moved the other patient out of the room so that we as a family could have the room to ourselves.

The last days of Alzheimer's are the meanest, ugliest and toughest to endure. The patient can no longer swallow and take in food or water, so it's a painful death to experience. I was not prepared for the pain we would endure, but my mom, my sister and I took turns and lovingly held Dad in our arms, doing everything we could to keep him comfortable. He was gasping for life as his lungs, heart and kidneys were weakening. We watched as his body began dehydrating and each organ started shutting down one by one. It was important to keep the oxygen mask over his face. It seemed to help him with the discomfort. He kept fighting to live because he didn't know enough to realize that God was taking him home.

"You don't have to fight any more, Harry Dent," I would say. "You are on your way to a much better place."

My father had fought and struggled through his entire life just to make it. Growing up in an alcoholic home during the Great Depression, he had learned what it meant to struggle— determination to win became a lifelong habit for him. And here he was, in the midst of the biggest struggle of his life, not knowing he did not need to struggle.

Dad made it through that night; the next night would prove to be even worse. I sat with him, holding his hand and holding his oxygen mask in place. As the night weighed heavily on, I began singing his favorite hymns and songs including "Amazing Grace," "It is Well with My Soul" and, of course, "People Need the Lord." These songs appeared to give him comfort as the spiritual light in his soul was still flickering.

And I spoke to him as if he knew who I was: "Harry Dent, you don't need to fight anymore. You are going home. You are just a visitor here. Your body is feeble and frail, but soon it will be restored. We will miss you, but we will join you one day. So don't fight anymore—just fly to Jesus."

I fully expected each laboring breath to be his last, but he kept on fighting. That was my dad, a fighter to the end. And a freedom fighter most of all. Now he struggled just to breathe. After missing two nights' sleep, I left the next morning to sleep in my own bed and to restore my grief-worn body. I kissed his brow, sensing it might be the last time I would see him, but hoping to return the next day to see him through to the end. But that kiss upon his brow would be my last. Later that night, while my sister and her son Blake were with him, Harry Dent graduated to heaven. Only then did he experience pure, ultimate freedom.

My sister called to give me the news of his passing, and I was numb. I had prayed for his passing, but I had been living on adrenalin. Now I was overwhelmed. It was just too hard to believe it was finally over. Then I thought, *No more sorrow, no more pain, no more confusion. Thank You, Jesus; Your child, my father, is finally safely home.* We were relieved for him, but still, it was devastating for us. I longed to see my dad as I had known him before with his bubbly personality and his eternal optimism. I still wish for that today. In my memories, I will always picture him that way.

As a family we made it through the long dark tunnel together. Through the tears and the stabbing pain, we made it. And to this day, none of us has ever forgotten what the Lord did for my father. No matter what the hurt or pain, we must never forget what God has done for us.

*   *   *   *   *

"I will remember the deeds of the Lord; yes, I will remember your miracles of long ago. I will meditate on all your works and consider all your mighty deeds. Your ways, O God, are holy. What god is so great as our God?" (Ps. 77:11–13).

23

THE LIGHT
AT THE END
OF THE TUNNEL

The greatest tribute a man can be given is the eulogy of his entire family. No one can attest to the character of someone more than those who knew him best. It's not easy standing and speaking before a large crowd of people at an emotional time, but each one of the Dent family felt compelled to do so, including my dear mother.

In a day and age when half of all marriages end in divorce and over 50 percent of children are born to single-parent families, a good husband and father is hard to find. Many dignitaries, such as former Governors David Beasley and James Edwards and Congressman Joe Wilson, as well as many friends could have spoken eloquent words at my father's service, but we decided to limit those words to his wife and four children. We did receive the pulpit flowers given by Billy Graham.

The Dent family eulogies were similar in that we all called my dad a "man of integrity" who was a wonderful husband and father. My father had eventually realized that his family was his first mission field, and he was right. The Bible asks the right question: What good will it be for a man if he gains the whole world, yet forfeits his soul?" (Matt. 16:26). And what good would it be for that man to lose his family?

As the family goes, so goes our nation. Today more than ever we need men and women to be role models for their children, building strong family units. God gave us the family as a model of holy love and a safe place to grow up, and unfortunately today we are witnessing the decline of this invaluable institution.

Recent research shows that divorce and unwed childbearing cost US taxpayers at least $112 billion each year.[1] Monetarily, the costs even dwarf the $104 billion price tag on the Iraq War.[2] Spiritually, the costs are incalculable. The rate of decline of the American family is a sad thing indeed for our country.

My father left specific instructions about what should be done after his death. His body was to be donated to the Medical University of South Carolina, and his memorial service was to be held at—yes, the "forbidden place"! Since his last act of service was to donate his body to science, there would be no casket. My father had also requested that Robertson McQuilkin, the former president of Columbia International University, preach at his memorial service.

My mother and I chose the music. Dad's favorite hymns were played before the service began, and a recorded tape of me singing his favorite song, "People Need the Lord," was played before the family appeared. Beth Greer sang "Were it Not for Grace," which was such a fitting song for this service, for we all knew the grace that had been given to my dad by the Lord Himself.

We never thought my mother would be able to do it, but she spoke first. She and my father had been committed to each other since high school. We watched as Mom confidently spoke from her heart as if giving a simple fireside chat about the most important man in her life. It was a supernatural event for a widow to be able to speak like that at her own husband's memorial service. It was the last thing she could do for the one person who had stood by her side and been her soul mate for some sixty years.

She started by saying that my father would have loved to be at his own funeral to see each one of his dear friends and family. Dad had always believed there was a peephole in heaven, and Mom told everyone she felt that he was watching the service.

She spoke about how CIU had made Harry a better man, and how my parents both believed that a real difference could be made if they could bring the entire world to the CIU campus. My parents were never the same after what they had learned there, and that is why my father chose the CIU chapel as the place for his memorial service.

My parents had both grown up in alcoholic and broken homes. They decided very early in their marriage that neither alcohol nor divorce would be part of their lives. My father was an ideologue from the time my mother first met him. He was a freedom fighter who was always interested in politics. After he gave his life to the Lord, however, he was not devoted to politics anymore—he participated like any red-blooded American, but he stopped committing eighty hours a week.

Harry Dent's favorite verses were found in Second Timothy: "All Scripture is God-breathed and is useful for teaching, rebuking, correcting and training in righteousness, so that the man of God may be thoroughly equipped for every good work" (3:16–17). My father had never applied the Bible to his life in this way until the age of forty-eight. After he came to know the Lord, he learned that applying God's Word in our lives was what would enable us to fulfill God's mission for us on this earth. He believed that each one of us was called to be a minister right where we lived.

Even though Dad's illness had sorely tested us, my mother stressed the point that we were not angry with God. The righteous have never been, and never will be, forsaken. Our family had also learned, partly through Dad's life, that good works cannot get anyone into heaven. Heaven opens when we bow our knees to Jesus Christ as Lord and Savior. Once my father learned that, he began to call the Bible the "Manufacturer's Handbook," and at a later stage in his life, he dedicated himself to studying it and teaching it from Genesis to Revelation. My mother's eulogy was a sermon that day, and my father would have been proud.

My brother, Harry Jr., espoused my father as a role model

who always helped others, loved kids and whom he most admired for his goodness. He explained how our father's character and integrity had helped all of us to have character ourselves. The naiveté about people that all my siblings possessed was due to our thinking that everyone had the character and integrity of our parents.

Yes, our father made his mark in politics and helped the South to have a voice nationally, but my brother stated that Dad would be more known for his stand for freedom. My brother wondered if the world would ever understand the impact my father had made in helping Romania emerge into freedom politically and religiously. Eugen Stancel told my brother before the service that of all the people who had come to help Romania from the US, Harry Dent was the most admired and revered man among the Romanian people. My brother travels the world to speak and to promote his books, and he constantly runs into people who track him down to express how Dad influenced their lives. Trent Lott told my brother that "unlike some men he knew who were great strategists, Harry Dent was a great political strategist *and* a great man."

My sister Dolly praised the legacy of my parents and presented my father as an example of the purpose-driven life, even before Rick Warren wrote the book. Dad was passionate about politics, but when he became God's man and was obedient to God's calling, he became more passionate about ministry than he ever had been about politics. He never wanted to waste one minute of his time while serving God. Now he had finally finished the race. My sister quoted what Billy Graham said in his book, *Billy Graham: God's Ambassador*, about his own impending death: "Someday you will read or hear that I am dead. Don't you believe a word of it! I shall be more alive then than I am now. I will just have changed my address."[3] And that could certainly be said of my dad. He has gone into the presence of God, whom he faithfully served. And there is no better place to be.

My brother Jack brought the most humor when he admitted that Dad had never been very fashionable; sometimes we had needed to protect him from the press. On the subject of my dad's sense of style, anyway, we could always agree with the *Washington Post*. To Jack, my father had been a family man who made time for his children. He just wondered when Dad had ever had downtime for himself. Our father was a man with a big heart, and that was the legacy he passed down to us.

I Never Dreamed

I was the last in the lineup. I don't normally speak or sing at funerals, because I tend to cry at the drop of a hat. It was a miracle that I was not drenched in tears. I mean an absolute miracle. But I had known, since that time in Romania when the Lord had reminded me of what He had done for my father and my family, that I would express my gratitude when Dad passed on. Here is what I said:

> We the children of Betty and Harry Dent consider it a privilege to be called their children. We have been truly blessed by the lives of our parents, who have always been there for us and provided us with a safe and secure marriage, as well as serving as living examples of character, even through difficult times. Although they were both products of alcoholic and dysfunctional homes, they made sure that life for us would be different. They were determined we would not endure some of the same trials and tribulations they had faced.
>
> I can remember so vividly asking the Lord in my college years to save my father because he was such a good person, and I loved him so much. That was a young girl's simple, but heartfelt prayer. I am grateful and thankful the Lord answered my prayer. Not only did He answer it, but He went way beyond that little girl's prayer. I never dreamed my father would give up his legal and political career and enter full-time Christian ministry with my mother at forty-eight years of age. I never dreamed he would attend the one place he had forbidden me to go, CIU, and come to love it as he did. I never dreamed he would attain the award of alumni of the year or ask to have his

memorial service here in this special place. I never dreamed he would minister all over the world, especially in the country of Romania. I think the thing he feared the most when I went to CIU was that I might become something gosh-awful like a missionary. What he didn't know was that the Lord would use him to be a missionary to many people.

After he became a Christian, the Lord graciously allowed my dad to live twenty-five more years in service to Him. He has lived to know intimately all of his grandchildren, and to be a part of their lives as well.

Although it is hard for us to be without him, we are thankful the Lord allowed us to have him for seventy-seven years. Serving the Lord turned out to be his greatest accomplishment, especially his work in Romania. And yes, as that plaque I placed under his pillow said, he did fulfill the meaning and purpose of life—to serve God. He lived his *dash*, that time between life and death, to the fullest.

About nine years ago, the Lord impressed upon my heart that it was time for me to go with my father to Romania to be a part of what he was doing there. My sister, Dolly, also felt that same call. In my heart, I felt his time of traveling to Romania would be ending soon, and this might be his last trip. It was a wonderful experience to be able to sing and speak with him in churches in Romania and see the fruits of his ministry. However, many nights I would lay my head on my pillow and cry myself to sleep. I knew in my spirit the Lord was preparing me for changes that would take place. He kept reminding me of a promise I made to Him before my father became a Christian—that if the Lord would save him, I would not be angry when He called him home. The Lord kept reminding me, "Do not forget what I have done for your family." And we have not forgotten.

I did not know those changes would be through a disease called Alzheimer's, which quickly diminished my father's brilliant mind and often left him confused. Although in the last few years he didn't always know who we were, or who he was or what he did in life, two things remained constant during most of his illness: he knew who Jesus was and he could always say the most wonderful blessings—yes, he could pray, even when he could barely speak, and he always took delight in doing so.

And so we, his family, who loved and adored him, give him back to the heavenly Father who so generously gave him to us. May his soul and mind rest in Him. We, his family, choose to remember the wonderful years of our loved one's life, when he was spirited, brilliant, so giving and loving, a man of integrity who set out to make a difference in this world and who made a difference through serving the King of kings and the Lord of lords. He was a man who learned that *the purpose of life is to serve God.* Although he served senators and presidents, he would be the first to tell you serving God was the most rewarding work of his life, and the benefits are out of this world! My father knew at age forty-eight that he needed the Lord, and he wanted to be a part of making sure the world around him knew about the Savior.

My father was always known as the big-picture man, and he would want us to see the big picture here today. Romans 8:18 speaks of suffering and ultimate glory: "For I consider that the sufferings of this present time are not worthy to be compared with the glory which shall be revealed in us" (NKJV). And in Second Corinthians 4:16–18, we read this: "Therefore, we do not lose heart. Even though our outward man is perishing, yet the inward man is being renewed day by day. For our light affliction, which is but for a moment, is working for us a far more exceeding and eternal weight of glory, while we do not look at the things which are seen, but at the things which are not seen. For the things which are seen are temporary, but the things which are not seen are eternal" (NKJV).

Eternity is what matters, and Harry Dent is no longer bound by a decayed body and mind. He is free in his heavenly home. Even though our hearts are filled with sorrow and we have grieved over time, yet *joy cometh in the morning* for we know he has a new body. His mind has been restored, and we know *we shall see him again on the other side.* To God be the glory!

I closed my eulogy with "We Shall See You Soon Again," a song Evie Tournquist Karlson sang at her father's funeral. And I sang it in voice and in sign language.

The Final Sendoff

At the end of the service, my mother was presented with two flags. The United States flag was presented by Lamar Brown, a veteran and a faithful friend, for my father's service in the Korean War and the National Guard. Eugen Stancel from Romania presented my mother with the Romanian flag.

Robertson McQuilkin, one of the men who spent many hours discipling my father, gave the final sendoff. Robertson compared my father to Daniel, the biblical prophet who served the leaders of three empires just as my father had served a senator and three presidents. Daniel served from the southern territory, like my father served from the southern region of the United States. Daniel and my father were both men of great courage and integrity. Daniel was a great man of the Book and a man of prayer; my father became a man of the Book and a man of prayer after he surrendered his life to God at age forty-eight. Both men served God's purpose and were men of hope. They both looked forward to serving in the final kingdom, which will never be destroyed.

As a family, we survived the dark tunnel of Alzheimer's, and we did find the light at the end of the tunnel. That light was my father's going home to heaven.

This present life is just the training ground for our new life in eternity. Harry Dent would be the first to tell you that he was a blessed man, for now he is in the presence of the Lord. And as my father always said, "Serve the Lord for your reward in heaven, where the retirement benefits are out of this world."

My father spent the last twenty-five years of his life making sure that all the people in the pews understood the important message that he missed for his first forty-eight years. He learned that the purpose of life is serving God, and that there is no greater calling. His tombstone reads:

Harry Shuler Dent, Sr.
February 21, 1930–September 28, 2007
He served a US Senator,
Three US Presidents,
And
THE KING OF KINGS AND LORD OF LORDS

Harry Dent left behind a legacy that can be seen today in his children and his grandchildren, in the books he wrote, in the ministries he started and in the lives he influenced. Although my father has "graduated" ahead of me, one day I will join him.

Life is so much more than the here and now. What really matters are the things we do that count for eternity. At age forty-eight my father went to the desert—CIU—and learned all he could to serve the purpose God had for him. That purpose went far beyond his daughter's prayers, and I will always be grateful. I had only wanted to make sure I would see my father in heaven—the rest was icing on the cake. God's main purpose for my dad will always be clearly seen in his life as a father and a grandfather, and in his work in the country of Romania.

24

ONE
LAST
DANCE

Since my father's passing, I have often wondered what he would say about what is happening in America today. He went into politics to save the world from Communism and to protect our freedoms. In time, he realized that politics could not save a person's soul and that only true freedom is in Jesus Christ. As the economy struggles, deficits skyrocket, and the enemy is at our gates, it is evident that politics in and of itself cannot save this county.

People are crying out for change and looking to politicians or to a political party to rescue us from our problems. But as we slide down a slippery slope with no end in sight, it is not necessarily politics that must change. It is the people who must change. And change must come from the inside out. Our problems are too numerous for any individual or party to solve. Our country is heading in the wrong direction. I wonder what our forefathers would do if they were in control today.

Freedom—A Precious Gift

It was one of those weekends, and the 11:00 p.m. news had just unnerved me. The terror alert was high; crime continued to rage; Iran and North Korea were again rearing their ugly heads; our government was bailing out the auto industry and trying

241

to control our healthcare; the economic indicators were down; the stock market was continuing to drop; oil was spewing uncontrollably from the Gulf of Mexico; and several states were headed toward bankruptcy. Was there anything positive to report? It didn't seem so tonight.

I was exhausted and lay down. My mind seemed to be replaying the negative reports. In frustration I called out to my dad.

"You left us here while the America you fought and struggled for is slowly crumbling from within."

I looked up, and sitting in the chair right before me was my dear sweet dad. He looked strong and had an unmistakable glow. He was no longer struggling between life and death—and he knew who I was. Then he rose from the chair and held his arms out as if he wanted to dance. My dad had always been a great dancer. He met my mom while dancing, and there was nothing he enjoyed more than dancing with one of his girls. It was always a treat to dance with Dad.

"Oh, Daddy," I said as he put his arm gently on my waist and held my hand in his. "We all miss you so much. We're still a little numb from losing you. But we see you all around us in the ministries you started, the words you wrote and the lives you touched."

I couldn't help but notice the touch of his hands. There were no longer cold. I could tell by the grip of his hands that he really knew I was his Sassy Pooh-pooh. I sensed the beat in his glide as he waltzed me around the room with that father-like twinkle in his eyes. I hadn't seen that sparkle in years. There was music playing in the background, a kind of music I had never heard before. It was as if we were dancing to a new beat.

I told him all about a trip I had taken to Romania in 2008 and how the believers there are continuing to grow and plant additional churches. I told him about the heart center and that they remembered him and appreciated all he did to help them.

"Amen," he said. "I am happy they are close to your heart,

too. And how about my wonderful grandchildren?"

I told him about his oldest grandchild Josh graduating from Charleston Southern University and marrying Sydney, a talented photojournalist. I told him about the twins—Jonathan, now working in business after graduating from University of South Carolina, and Harrison, who is graduating from law school next week and has his grandfather's love for fighting for what he believes this country needs. Most importantly, I told him that they are striving to put their faith first in their lives.

I told him about Dolly's boys who are all excelling with their gifts and talents. Blake just got married to Anna Creech and graduated with an MBA. Clay is in New York City working in the financial world after graduating with honors from USC. And then I told him about Graham and his calling to the mission field.

"Wow, my heart is so touched about Graham," my dad said with a tear in his eye, "and I am proud of all of them."

Then I told him about Jack's children. How Lizy is majoring in political science and history at the University of Miami in Ohio and how she was engaged to Dave Huff, who is serving our country in Afghanistan. Sarah, so pretty and tall, is beginning to visit colleges and plan her future. And of course, I told him about his namesake, Harry II, whose athletics and charming personality are his biggest assets.

I told him how Harry Jr. has another book on the *New York Times* bestseller list and that many of the things he predicted years ago are coming true, like the perfect storm that is coming our way.

"He was always a big-picture man in the financial world, like I was in the political world. Like father, like son."

Then he asked me, "How is my dancing girl?"

I told him she will never be the same and that his death had been a tough adjustment for her, yet she volunteers at the hospital and at CIU, and goes to Bible studies.

And then I asked him what he thought of America—the one

his two brothers had died for while defending our freedoms. I told him how things are changing quickly, how we seem powerless to stop it and how this generation is taking their freedoms for granted, not realizing we could lose them. Oh, how I want him here to think of some kind of strategy!

"Yes, dear, things are changing. That is what happens when a nation becomes so prosperous. The people tend to forget the principles, hard work and sacrifices that brought them that prosperity. Most importantly, they tend to forget the hand of God that provided all those blessings. Sassy-pooh, God has not changed. He never changes. He is the same yesterday, today and tomorrow. It is America that has changed."

I told him how we've taken God out of everything. Years ago we took prayer out of schools. Today some people want to remove references to God from our national monuments, and they are trying to eliminate the words "under God" from our pledge. It's just a matter of time before we erase "In God we Trust" from our money. In some places, they're even removing the Ten Commandments.

"Oh, how I hoped days like this would never come," he responded.

I told him some of the positive things, telling him how we had elected the first African American president, who had also come from a broken home and overcome so many obstacles. He is truly a product of our American democracy. I told him how African Americans had come a long way since the Nixon era and that now even the Republican National Committee has elected an African American as its chairman.

"I'm happy for my black brothers and sisters who have longed for this day. Ginny, pray for your president, pray for your leaders—never let a day go by that you do not lift them up in prayer.

"There are no Republicans and Democrats here. There simply is not the need for man's ways when God is on His throne."

I told him I would certainly pray for our president and our

country, but that I was discouraged because everything he had fought for is now being threatened. I told him how the government is taking control of so many things: the car industry, the education system, the banking industry and healthcare.

"Freedom is the most precious gift that has been given to America," Dad replied. "But the price of those earthly freedoms has been paid for by the blood of those who were willing to stand. If succeeding generations are not willing to stand for freedom, you will not continue to have the freedoms my generation enjoyed so immensely. All who desire freedom must stand together: men and women, black and white, young and old, Democrat and Republican, Independent and Libertarian—regardless of creed or color. Don't forget that your democratic form of government, your laws and the Constitution are still in place. You still have your right to vote, to run for office, to speak out on issues and to bring grievances to the courts. A democracy is not perfect, but it is still the best form of government on earth. It works best when people have virtues which come from one's faith."

I told him how we were turning into a greedy nation of people who don't ask what they can do for their country—they ask what their country can do for them. How we were like pigs eating at the trough. I told him that we have doubled the number of citizens receiving government benefits since the 1950s, and that we have no idea that the more control the government takes, the less freedom we will have in the end. I told him how the Romanian pastors had asked me why we as a country were so bent on adopting a system that they were so glad to be throwing off. And I told him how the South Carolina Senator Jim DeMint said that just like Odysseus in Homer's *Odyssey* could not resist the siren song, "we are falling for the siren song of socialism, and it already has many Americans under its control."[1]

"Karl Marx himself knew a democracy could not survive in the end," replied my father. "Marx said, 'A democracy will succeed until its citizens discover they can vote themselves money from the treasury, then they will bankrupt it.'"

I told him how I understood why he fought so hard for states' rights as a counterbalance to the power of the federal government.

"Yes," he said. "The federal government can grow into a monster—if the people let it. Your leaders must reduce government dependency if your nation is to survive.

"You know, honey," he went on, "we used to discuss the rise and fall of a nation, and America is following those steps just as other civilizations have. We tend to forget that Rome and Greece collapsed from within. America could do the same.

"Pray for your nation—pray with a passion—just as you did for me."

I told him how our beloved Washington is a mess and how there are Watergates all around us in business and government—yet no one seems to care. I told him how our national debt is approaching $12 trillion and our own destructive behavior adds up to $2 trillion yearly.[2]

"Ginny," Dad said, "above all, remember that this world as we know it is not our home. Heaven is our home. While you live on earth, you're only a pilgrim. A theocracy is the best form of government, and I am enjoying it now. There is nothing like it on earth. You are seeing so many things crumbling around you, but do not be afraid. Never forget you are part of an everlasting kingdom that will never crumble, a kingdom that will never end. As the Bible says in the book of Revelation, there will be a new heaven and a new earth. Words cannot describe what true spiritual freedom and life eternal in the presence of God are like. I only *thought* I was free in America. Here, I am bound by nothing—I have total bliss, total freedom, total worship, total harmony.

"One more piece of advice to my little girl," he whispered. "Remember what Dwight Moody said: 'The world is a sinking ship, and your job is to get people off the ship before the ship goes down.' You will not be able to repair all the leaks in the ship, and the ship is in pretty bad shape right now. The Bible told us it would be.

"It is up to each believer to be a light to those around them. Only God knows, dear, what will happen to America. Remember, He is in control. And take care of my dancing girl."

Let Your Light Shine

I heard the sound of music in the background . . .

Just knowing You sets me free,
And the plans You have for me.
When all is lost,
Your hand I'll trust;
You deliver me.

You hold this world
In the palm of Your hand
You're the only hope I need;
Through sinking sands
My faith will stand;
You are all I need . . .

The precious last dance with my father suddenly began to fade away as a persistent blaring brought me back to reality. The music I had heard in my dream was now filling the bedroom as the radio continued its wake-up call.

"Honey," I heard Alton say, "Get up and turn off that alarm. It's time to get up.

"Alton, you mean, you mean . . . it was just a dream?' I asked in a confused state.

"Welcome back to the real world, dear."

"You would never believe who was in my dream! It was so real. I did not want to wake up. I was dancing with my dad. And that song—it was there too. We can still be the beacon light to the world as the ship goes down, can't we dear?"

"You are back in your dream now. We're barely giving off a flicker right now. At the rate we're going, that flicker may soon be gone."

"Don't ever say that! We must always be a light to the world—a shining light sitting on the hill—even as the ship goes down."

"Honey, where have you been? America is not what she used to be. She has so many holes, we can't plug them all."

"We can't, but if we turn back to God—He can. I won't give up on Him. And I will pray with a passion for this country that I love. My daddy is in heaven where the benefits are out of this world. When I finally get there, we will experience true freedom together. Until then, I must fulfill my mission on earth. But until God calls me home, I will not give up on this country, and I do not give up easily!"

"Amen!" I heard from a distant heaven. "That's my Sassy Pooh-pooh."

EPILOGUE

ROMANIA
IN
2010

Romania has come a long way since Nicolae Ceauşescu ran the country. The government has relaxed a lot of its control and offers more freedom of expression, including religious worship. The US and Romania signed a treaty in December of 2005 authorizing a permanent American military presence on Romanian soil. In cooperation with the Romanian military, the United States is currently building two American military bases in their country. One is located in Babadag, and the other is an air base located near Constanza. I sense these agreements were influenced by all the Americans who offered assistance to Romania in the 1990s.

In order to be eligible for membership with the European Union, Romania was required to step up reform for human rights and freedom of expression, and they had to set up democratic systems and a free-market economy. These requirements have been met in the years since Ceauşescu's reign. Romania joined the European Union on January 1, 2007, and this has provided much needed aid for their people. The country also hopes to adopt the euro by the year 2014. Even with these accomplishments, Romania still has a long way to go to improve its infrastructure and economy. Of the countries represented in the European Union, Romania and Bulgaria are by far the poorest, averaging only 33 percent gross domestic product (GDP) compared to the other countries.

Christianity has also made great strides in many Romanian villages. Although there are Romanian Orthodox Churches on virtually every corner, and the 2002 census showed that the country was about 87 percent Romanian Orthodox, the goal of the evangelical church in Romania is to plant an evangelical congregation in every village. For now, since it takes money to plant a church and since poverty is still prevalent in the villages, many villages are left without an evangelical witness. But the church continues to grow.

*   *   *   *   *

My father never returned to Romania after he received honorary citizenship in July of 1999 for all his work there. He was beginning his decline at that time, but even so, the ministry to Romania continued with donations from faithful believers and the help of John and Margie Simmons, Jesse Powers and Bobbie Horton Caldwell.

In 2008 I felt led to return to the country my father had loved. While there I was asked to speak and sing in churches. I also shared what had happened to my father. I was able to see many of the churches my father's ministry had assisted in building, and I spent time with many of the pastors that Laity Alive and Serving helped train and put in place. Since the fall of Communism, the number of churches in the city of Cluj has increased from three to eight, and the surrounding villages continue to build churches as financial provisions are received.

On that trip I visited the Heart Institute in Cluj and was able to see, at a distance, heart surgeries being conducted. I was able to speak with one of the top cardiologists from Cluj, who had come to Providence Hospital in Columbia for training. He was most appreciative for the opportunity he had been given.

On June 22, 2008, I was able to attend the opening of a new Baptist church in the village of Alunis. The church dedication was attended by over four hundred people, with seating for only two hundred. Consistent with Romanian church dedication services, it lasted four and a half hours!

While I was there, a bus showed up with fourteen members of Faith Baptist Church from Swansea, South Carolina. Pastor David Carter and his wife, Cathy, had brought this group to be part of the dedication. Faith Baptist Church is a small but powerful church that, along with Jesse Powers' ministry, had helped in the building of this new place of worship. I was touched that these people had given so sacrificially. Then I discovered that Faith Baptist had already raised more money to help build another church in a nearby village. These people certainly qualified as "Romaniacs."

At the new church dedication, there was standing room only. Villagers peered in windows to see what the celebration was all about. On the podium and outside the church stood two flags—one Romanian and one American. These flags were symbolic of the partnership, which continues today, between Romanian Baptists and USA Baptists. What a celebration it was for this village to finally have an evangelical church in its midst after all these years.

According to Patrick Johnstone and Jason Mandryk, authors of *Operation World*, Romania has Europe's third highest percentage of evangelicals, just behind the United Kingdom and Latvia. The book reports, "Romania has seen a substantial church planting movement with an average of five new churches being built every week until 1999."[1] The authors believe that a lack of human and material resources has prevented this rate from continuing after 1999.[2] During my recent visit almost all the village churches where I spoke had experienced decline in membership. Romanians were moving to countries such as Italy, Spain and the USA due to unemployment. This diaspora is helpful for spreading the gospel in Italy and Spain and America, but it's hard on the churches in Romania.

Bible training for existing and future pastors remains a great need. The average pastor still has three to five churches to over-see, and there are new believers requesting preachers to come and plant churches in their homes. One Sunday Eugen's wife Vali and I traveled with a village pastor, and I spoke and sang in three of his five churches; we left at 6:00 a.m. and returned at midnight. It must be exhausting being a circuit-riding preacher. But there are not enough human resources to fill the needs. My visit left me feeling that there is still much more to do, and so little time.

North Greenville University (NGU), located in Tigerville, South Carolina, is answering the call. While I was in Romania, Dr. Don Dowless, vice president of academic affairs, and Dr. Gerald Roe, associate professor of intercultural studies/missions, were there as well, working to establish a new partnership with the Baptists in Cluj. This relationship is now focused on train-ing pastors to establish an institute for biblical training. Such an effort will provide much-needed training for future leaders and inspire them to reach out and do mission work in neighbor-ing countries. My father would be pleased to know that NGU has stepped up to the plate for the pastors in the country he so dearly loved.

I could see my father everywhere I went in Romania; it's a country that will always be close to my family's heart.

CONCLUSION

When we lose someone we love, we always want that last dance. My mom and I continue to talk with my dad in dreams, and he is always in our memories. I know him and I know his thoughts, just as if he were here.

Our lives are a journey. The end is usually far from where we began. Even though my father was a freedom fighter from his earliest days, the face of his efforts changed over the years: His early career was spent physically fighting for freedom through the Korean War; he was willing to give his life to secure freedoms for his country. He went on to fight intellectually, serving many years in the United States Capitol, while Lady Liberty stood high above its dome as a constant reminder that this country values freedom above all. As noble as his intentions were, the freedom he was fighting for was external and temporal. He later found that true, lasting freedom only comes when we surrender our lives to Jesus, who is preeminent above all things, and at that point he began to fight spiritually. That gradual process toward true freedom continues, for all who will receive it, through the power of the Holy Spirit until the day the Lord calls us home. Our freedom is to be used for His glory, not our own. When we graduate to heaven, the transformation will be complete. "It is for freedom that Christ has set us free" (Gal. 5:1).

My journey into spiritual freedom began when I was sixteen, and it has taken me from the height of modeling and materialism to ministering in the developing countries of this world. My dad's spiritual journey began when he was forty-eight. His life was a journey from the marble columns of power and the American dream to the countryside of Eastern Europe. Dad quickly surpassed me in his journey toward true spiritual freedom. It gives me great comfort to know that now he is totally free and that one day I'll be totally free as well. Heavenly freedom is the kind that one cannot earn, because Jesus already paid for it in full. And it can never be taken away. We all yearn for something greater; we have a spiritual hunger for something we cannot seize on earth. Temporal things cannot bring inner peace; but once on the path toward Christ, we can experience true peace found only in Him.

Earthly freedoms are different from spiritual ones. If we are not willing to stand and fight for the freedoms we enjoy here, we simply won't have them. I'll never forget what an official from the Czech Republic once said to my husband and me. The Czech government had invited us to come and help them improve deaf education. A few weeks into our visit, as we traveled around their country, I made a comment to an official: "I'm amazed at how well preserved are all your monuments, cathedrals and historic buildings," I said. "Your country does not appear to have the massive damage that neighboring countries received from Hitler during World War II."

"Oh, there is good reason for that," he replied. "When Hitler and the German forces crossed into our borders, we simply threw our arms up, surrendered and said, 'Take us.' We were simply too scared to fight.'"

I was stunned at his honesty. Deep inside I hoped that my America would never be cowardly. As an American and the daughter of a veteran, I pray for the preservation of our freedoms. Instead of just throwing my arms up and saying, "Oh, well, come what may," I am willing to stand for those liberties. They are not passed down. Each generation must stand against tyranny to preserve its individual freedoms. As Ronald Reagan said:

> Freedom is never more than one generation away from extinction. We didn't pass it to our children in the bloodstream. It must be fought for, protected and handed on for them to do the same, or one day we will spend our sunset years telling our children and children's children what it was once like in the United States when men were free.[1]

My father and I both saw the courage of many people who were denied freedoms by their government and yet who risked their lives to pursue liberty. We fellowshiped with the underground believers in Romania, and we saw places where many had been beaten and some killed. We both witnessed the bold actions of the underground church in China. I personally saw believers in the Middle East who risked everything to proclaim the name of Christ. Today many people continue risking their lives by tunneling, boating, flying or packing themselves into a crate for a chance at earthly freedoms. People in oppressive countries only want what we so freely enjoy. Those who risk it all to possess it never want to go back.

We must never lose what made us the most powerful and envied nation in the world. We must never stop being a "beacon on the hill." While the stand for freedom must begin with each of us individually, one alone is not enough. All freedom lovers must stand together. In my heart I still believe there are men and women who will stand for freedom, just as my father did—not out of pride or power, but out of a sense of service to God and the people of this nation.

Spiritual freedom has already been paid for and preserved for us by the blood of Jesus on the cross. One simply needs to accept it. When you have freedom in Christ you are forever secure in that freedom. My life verse is Matthew 6:33, which compels me to "seek first his kingdom and his righteousness"—but the earthly part of me will always be my daddy's little girl.

As Chuck Colson so boldly stated, "There is too much of the world in the church and not enough of the church in the world."[2] But I have hope for this country, because the Scriptures tell us it is never too late to turn back to God. Change begins with each one of us.

When people see Jesus authentically demonstrated in our lives and they smell His sweet aroma in us, only then can we make a difference in this world.

The Bible reminds us: "If my people, who are called by my name, will humble themselves and pray and seek my face and turn from their wicked ways, then will I hear from heaven and will forgive their sin and heal their land" (2 Chron. 7:14).

How I pray that we as a nation would fast, pray and kneel before the Father before it is too late. Avery Willis outlines the *The Seven Stages in the Judgment of God:*

1. God convicts of sin;
2. God sends warnings;
3. God allows people to experience the consequences of their sin;
4. God withdraws His presence;
5. God removes His hedge of protection;
6. God gives people over to their sin and its destruction;
7. God destroys the nation.[3]

Ann Graham Lotz, Billy Graham's daughter, said it another way when being interviewed after 9/11 on CBS's *The Early Show*. Jane Clayson asked her, "How could God let something like this happen?" She responded this way: "I believe that God is deeply saddened by this, just as we are, but for years we've been telling God to get out of our schools, to get out of our government and to get out of our lives, and being the gentle Father that He is, I believe that He has calmly backed out. How can we expect God to give us His blessing and His protection if we demand He leave us alone?"[4]

God has not changed—we are the ones who have changed.

And God is willing to forgive us at any time, if we will only turn back to Him. I pray we would be humble enough to do that, because we so desperately need Him.

* * * * *

I believe God has given this country our freedoms and wealth so that we can be a beacon to the world. With these blessings comes equal responsibility to use them for God's kingdom, not for our own selfish desires. The Bible clearly tells us that "from everyone who has been given much, much will be demanded" (Luke 12:48).

In our fast-paced society in which constant demands seem to shorten each day, we tend to neglect the life-changing power of prayer. Prayer involves confession, thanksgiving and supplication before God. God continues to intervene in the course of our lives and in our country when we pray. He wants us to be His children, to dance to His beat and not to our own. Prayer helps us do that. Never doubt that our heavenly Father listens and responds to our heartfelt prayers. I know that He responded to my prayers for my father when I was only seventeen years old. I had no idea that prayer would affect so many people. No matter what happens to our country, our power of prayer can never be taken away. It is only diminished when we fail to use it. At a time when our country is removing prayer from every part of our lives, it can never be removed from our hearts.

I will always remember with gratitude what my heavenly Father did as an answer to my simple prayer. He, and only He, has the best-made plans for our lives. I will be eternally grateful to Him and Him alone.

Freedom is a great paradox. God taught both my dad and me the meaning of true freedom. It lies not in conforming to the world's expectations, or even in obtaining what we believe to be our deepest wishes. Rather, Charles Colson defines freedom as "following the call of God on our lives."[5] We need only reach out and take His hand, and let Him lead in the dance of our lives.

ENDNOTES

Chapter 1: Childhood in Two Capitals

1. Harry S. Dent, *The Prodigal South Returns to Power* (New York: John Wiley and Sons, 1978), 61. (Hereafter referred to as Dent, *PSRP*)
2. Dent, *PSRP*, 59.
3. Dent, *PSRP*, 3.
4. Dent, *PSRP*, 66.
5. Dent, *PSRP*, 8.
6. Dent, *PSRP*, 69.
7. Van Hipp, "Souls and Politics," *State*, October 6, 2007, A11 Editorial.

Chapter 2: Coming into Our Own

1. Denis Noe, "The Attempted Assassination of George Wallace," *Crime Magazine*, September 14, 2003.
2. Dent, *PSRP*, 73.
3. Dent, *PSRP*, 121.
4. "RUMANIA: Enfant Terrible," *Time*, April 2, 1973.
5. Catherine Lovatt, "Ceausescu's Return" in *Central Europe Review*, August 23, 1999.
6. Ibid.

Chapter 3: Nixon and the South

1. Dent, *PSRP*, 136.
2. Dent, *PSRP*, 137.
3. Dent, *PSRP*, 166.
4. Essie Mae Washington-Williams and William Stadiem, *Dear Senator* (New York: HarperCollins, ReganBooks, 2005), 12.
5. Dent, *PSRP*, 166.
6. Patrick Buchanan, *Conservative Votes, Liberal Victories* (New York: Quadrangle/New York Times, 1975), 49–50.
7. Robert Charles Smith, *We Have No Leaders* (New York: State University of New York, 1996), 169.
8. Wilson Riles, "The Modesto Bee" in *Rafferty Post*, Thursday, May 21, 1970, A-10.
9. Barbara Kiviat, "The Social Side of Schooling" in *John Hopkins Magazine*, April 2000.
10. Dent, *PSRP*, 197.
11. Dent, *PRSP*, 177.
12. Paul Clancy, *Philadelphia Inquirer* in Dent, *PSRP*, 206.
13. Dent, *PSRP*, 207.
14. Dent, *PSRP*, 211.
15. William Safire, *Before the Fall* (New York: Doubleday, 1975), 203.

Chapter 5: Turning toward Home and Family

1. George Wallace in Dent, *PRSP*, 168.

Chapter 6: Watergate—The Beginning

1. Dent, *Cover Up* (San Bernardino, CA: Here's Life Publishers, 1986), 34.

Chapter 8: Of Boy Scouts and Honor

1. Dent, *PSRP*, 263.
2. James Polk, "Dent Put on Probation" in *Washington Star-News*, December 12, 1974.
3. Ibid.

4. Lee Brandy, *State*, December 1, 1974.

5. Polk, "Dent Put on Probation."

6. *Paul Harvey News*, December 19, 1974. In Lee Brandy's December 1, 1974 article for *State*, he wrote, "Attorneys in the Special Prosecutor's office are apparently bent on snaring any prize catch in sight."

7. Thomas Waring, ed., *Charleston Evening Post*, December 13, 1974.

8. Jack Anderson, "Loophole May Allow Food Shortages" in the *Washington Post*, November 22, 1974.

9. Leonard Garment, *In Search of Deep Throat* (New York: Basic Books, 2001), 9.

10. Uncle Wiggly, "More on the 'Deep Throat' Theory" in blog post at http://carolinasimpletruth.blogspot.com, February 8, 2005.

11. FBI Director J. Edgar Hoover's black-bag phone taps had secured his position with previous presidents. In fact, my father was present when Hoover notified Nixon that he wouldn't spy for him as he had for other presidents. Hoover was angry when Nixon and John Mitchell attempted to retire him because of his declining mental health. Among Hoover's staff it was an open secret that their boss needed to retire. (Dent, *PSRP*, 220–21.)

Chapter 9: Forbidden Knowledge and Path

1. Dent, *Cover Up*, 36.

Chapter 10: Just Can't Give It Up

1. Dent, *PSRP*, Foreword, vii.

2. Jack Anderson and Les Whitten, "Ford May Aid Watergate-Era Figures" in the *Washington Post*, August 14, 1975.

Chapter 11: The Final Surrender

1. Dent, *Cover Up*, 37.

2. Dent, *PSRP*, 238.

3. Dent, *PSRP*, 241.

4. Dent, *Cover Up*, 44.
5. Robert Semple Jr., "Nixon's Inner Circle" in the *New York Times*, August 3, 1969.
6. Dent, *PSRP*, 247.

Chapter 13: Expanding Horizons and New Opportunities

1. Dent, *Cover Up*, 37.
2. Bob McAlister, "Dent's Encounter with Real Power" in the *State,* October 3, 2007, A9.

Chapter 14: Social Concerns for the Sake of Christ

1. Lee Bandy, "Stricken Atwater Reorganizes Life, Priorities" in the *State*, November 2, 1990, 1-A.

Chapter 15: Teaming Up with the Persecuted Brethren in Romania

1. Jeffrey Simon and Hans Binnendijk, "Romania and NATO Membership Reassessment at the July 1997 NATO Summit," NDU Strategic Forum Number 101, February 1997.

Chapter 16: A Challenging Journey

1. Barbara Joiner, *The Story of Martha Myers* (Birmingham, AL: SBC Women's Missionary Union, 2005), 120.
2. Ibid., 11.

Chapter 17: The Real Heroes

1. Erich Bridges and Jerry Rankin, *Lives Given, Not Taken* (Richmond, VA: SBC International Mission Board, 2005), 75.
2. From the 1993 movie *Schindler's List*
3. Joiner, *The Story of Martha Myer*s, 78.
4. Ibid., 147.
5. Bridges and Rankin, *Lives Given, Not Taken*, 43.
6. Ibid., 38.
7. Ibid., 65.
8. Ibid., 69.
9. Rob Morse, "The Gospel According to John," *San Francisco Chronicle*, February 22, 2002.

Chapter 19: The Unexpected Tunnel

1. Jack Bass and Marilyn Thompson, *Ol' Strom* (Marietta, GA: Longstreet Press, 1998), 344.
2. William Rodman Shankle and Daniel G. Amen, *Preventing Alzheimer's* (New York: Berkeley, 2004), 1.

Chapter 20: Ongoing Changes and Challenges

1. From an interview with Dr. Jacobo Mintzer, Associate Director of Alzheimer's Research at the Medical University of South Carolina.
2. Alzheimer's Research and Prevention Foundation, http://alzheimersprevention.org, accessed May 18, 2010.
3. Dr. Dharma Singh Khalsa and Cameron Stauth, *Brain Longevity* (New York: Grand Central Publishers, 1999), 69.
4. Dr. Vincent Fortanasce, *The Anti-Alzheimer's Prescription* (New York: Gotham, 2008), 6.
5. Ibid., 9.
6. Ibid., 8.
7. Dr. Archibald Hart, *Adrenaline and Stress* (Nashville: W Publishing Group, 1995), 26–27
8. Washington-Williams and Stadiem, *Dear Senator,* 97.

Chapter 21: Ups and Downs

1. Senator Charles Schumer, actual words from the transcript of the Senate Judiciary Hearings, June 27, 2002, 755–56.

Chapter 23: The Light at the End of the Tunnel

1. Benjamin Scafidi, *The Taxpayer Costs of Divorce and Unwed Childbearing* (Institute for American Values, 2008).
2. Bryan Bender, "Cost of Iraq War nearly $2b a week" at http://www.boston.com/news/world/middleeast/articles/2006/09/28/cost_of_iraq_war_nearly_2b_a_week/.
3. Tehabi Books, comp., *Billy Graham: God's Ambassador* (New York: Time Life, 1999), 274.

Chapter 24: One Last Dance

1. Jim DeMint, *Saving Freedom* (Nashville: Fidelis Books, 2009), 44.
2. DeMint and J. David Woodard, *Why We Whisper* (Lanham, MD: Rowman and Littlefield, 2008), 148.

Epilogue: Romania in 2010

1. Patrick Johnstone and Jason Mandryk, *Operation World*, 21st Edition (Fort Washington, PA: WEC International, 2001), 536.
2. Ibid.

Conclusion

1. Ronald Reagan, Classic Quotes from the 40th President of the United States, www.quotationspage.com/quote/33739.html.
2. Colson, *Faith on the Line* (Colorado Springs: Cook, 1993).
3. From an unpublished sermon series by Dr. Avery Willis titled *The Pathway of God's Presence*.
4. Ann Graham Lotz, interview on CBS's *The Early Show* with Jane Clayson, September 13, 2001.
5. Charles Colson, *The Good Life* (Wheaton, IL: Tyndale, 2005), 29.

This book was produced by CLC Publications. We hope it has been life-changing and has given you a fresh experience of God through the work of the Holy Spirit. CLC Publications is an outreach of CLC Ministries International, a global literature mission with work in over fifty countries. If you would like to know more about us or are interested in opportunities to serve with a faith mission, we invite you to contact us at:

CLC Ministries International
PO Box 1449
Fort Washington, PA 19034

Phone: 215-542-1242
E-mail: orders@clcpublications.com
Website: www.clcpublications.com

DO YOU LOVE GOOD CHRISTIAN BOOKS?
Do you have a heart for worldwide missions?

You can receive a FREE subscription to
CLC's newsletter on global literature missions
Order by e-mail at:

clcworld@clcusa.org
Or fill in the coupon below and mail to:

**PO Box 1449
Fort Washington, PA 19034**

FREE *CLC WORLD* SUBSCRIPTION!

Name: _____

Address:_____

_____

Phone: _____ E-mail:_____

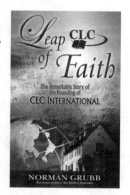

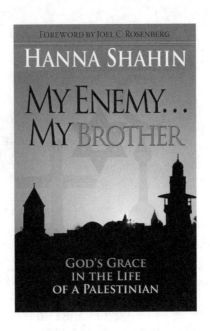

My Enemy. . . My Brother

Hanna Shahin

Read the incredible story of Hanna Shahin, a Palestinian boy raised in the old city of Jerusalem who was saved and transformed by the grace of God, then empowered to become a leading Christian broadcaster. His ministry has affected the lives of untold millions of listeners from Iraq on the east to Morocco on the west, and every country in between.

Trade paper ISBN-13: 978-0-87508-998-0

A Passion for Prayer
Tom Elliff

Of all the disciplines of the Christian life, prayer is perhaps the most neglected. Yet Jesus' brief earthly life was permeated with it. *A Passion for Prayer* seeks to help you develop—or deepen—your communion with God. Drawing on personal experience and God's Word, Pastor Tom Elliff shares principles for daily coming before the throne of grace.

Trade paper ISBN-13: 978-1-936143-03-0

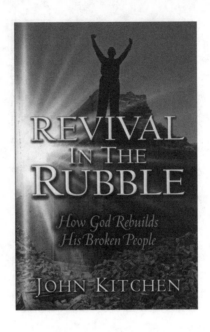

Revival in the Rubble

John Kitchen

How God Rebuilds His Broken People

Can spiritual life and renewal ever be found in the midst of rubble and devastation? "Yes!" says John Kitchen. "When God wants to do a fresh, reviving work in His people, He finds a person and breaks his heart."

Do you read of revivals in the past and find yourself asking God, "Why not here? Why not now? Why not me?"

If so, pick up this book now.

Trade paper ISBN-13: 978-0-87508-873-0

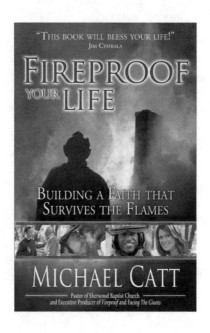

Fireproof Your Life
Michael Catt

Using illustrations from his own life and from the movie, *Fireproof*, Catt discusses practical issues such as temptation, marriage and finances, helping us build a faith that resists our corrosive culture. Rather than succumb to the pressure of circumstances, we can stand tall and face our challenges in Christ's power.

Life's trials can *overcome* us—or they can *serve* us, growing us into the mature, life-giving believers God intends.

Trade paper ISBN-13: 978-0-87508-984-3